Anonymous

Christian Lyrics

Chiefly selected from modern authors

Anonymous

Christian Lyrics
Chiefly selected from modern authors

ISBN/EAN: 9783744792684

Printed in Europe, USA, Canada, Australia, Japan

Cover: Foto ©Thomas Meinert / pixelio.de

More available books at **www.hansebooks.com**

Christian Lyrics:

CHIEFLY SELECTED FROM

MODERN AUTHORS.

> "Such songs have power to quiet
> The restless pulse of care—
> And come like the benediction
> That follows after prayer!"

Fourth Edition.

LONDON
HAMILTON, ADAMS, AND CO.
NORWICH: J. FLETCHER.

Preface.

In this little volume we have endeavoured to string together such Christian Lyrics as seem to us specially adapted to be the expression of home thoughts, and the companions of everyday life.

Mingled with many lyrics hitherto unpublished, or but little known, will be found some, the words of which have long been familiar to us all. If an excuse for this be needed, it must be found in the feeling, which we trust others will share, that—even were it not for their intrinsic beauty—they are enshrined in so many hearts, and consecrated by so many long-cherished and hallowed associations, that no collection of sacred poetry would be complete without them.

We have endeavoured, as far as possible, to print these lyrics in their original form: except in one or two instances, we have not knowingly omitted any of the verses; but should occasional incompleteness, or deviation from the true reading be detected, it must be accounted for by the difficulty of tracing some of these pieces to their source, and to the consequent necessity of trusting to collections, the editors of which have not felt themselves bound to be equally scrupulous.*

To those authors who have so willingly permitted us to insert their poems, and to Messrs. Longman and Co., who have allowed us to transfer some pieces from *Lyra Germanica*, we beg here to offer our deserved acknowledgments.

Should our little collection be of any service in suggesting sacred thoughts, or exciting holy feelings, we shall not regret that we have brought together, for the cheering of others' hearts, what has been such a source of joy and refreshing to our own.

---

* Since the publication of the second edition, our attention has been called to an error of the kind above referred to. The two verses of the poem beginning, "Still nigh me, O my Saviour, stand," page 112, are taken from hymns by different authors; the first is by Charles Wesley, and the second is part of a hymn translated from the German by John Wesley. The hymn in its present form was borrowed from a collection where it had grown dear and familiar to us, and as the pieces alluded to are too long to insert entire, we prefer retaining it as it is, hoping that its beauty will excuse this deviation from our rule.

Contents.

		PAGE.
The Sleep	E. B. Browning	1
The Peace of God	A. A. Procter	3
Prayer	R. C. Trench	5
The Cloud	Excelsior	6
The Ivy	C. Mackay	10
Onward	L. R.	12
Never hasting, never resting		13
Enoch	C. F. Alexander	15
For Ever		17
Buds and Blossoms	L. R.	17
The Suppliant	R. C. Trench	18
Strive, Wait, and Pray	A. A. Procter	20
Thou maintainest my lot	A. L. Waring	21
Lord, and what shall this man do?	Christian Year	22
Suspiria	Longfellow	23
Mortality	Poems, by Author of "John Halifax"	24
My Times are in Thy hand	A. L. Waring	25
Milton on his Blindness	E. Lloyd	27
Trust	Gerhardt	29
A Valediction	E. B. Browning	30
Abide with me	H. F. Lyte	31
To a Waterfowl	Bryant	33
The Alpine Gentian	Excelsior	34
The Golden Rule	S. A. Storrs	36

CONTENTS.

		PAGE.
It shall be returned to thee again	E. B. Browning	39
Strength, Love, and Rest	L. R.	39
Speak Gently		41
Think Gently of the Erring		42
Judge not	A. A. Procter	44
Faith, Hope, and Charity	Montgomery	45
Life's Lesson	Excelsior	45
The Streamlet's Song	L. R.	47
Hymn of the City	Bryant	50
Omnipresence	Bowring	52
The Brooklet	Sir R. Grant	52
A Morning Prayer	Lyra Germanica	54
The Second Day	Whytehead	56
The Bright and Morning Star		59
Heavenward	Lyra Germanica	60
The Building of the House	C. Mackay	62
How old art thou?		65
Thy way, not mine	Bonar	66
Resignation	Steele	67
Commit thy way to God	Paul Gerhardt	68
He doeth all things well	Anne Bronte	70
Love to God	I. A. E.	71
Undertake for me		73
The Promised One	Hankinson	74
Christmas Day	Christian Year	76
A Christmas Carol	E. H. Sears	78
Robins and their Songs	Excelsior	80
Make Thy face to shine upon Thy servant	Toplady	82
Lord, that I might receive my sight	Milman	83
Looking unto Jesus	Christian Exam.	84
Cast me not away from Thy presence	Heber	85
Pray without ceasing	Lord Morpeth	86
Let us pray	R. C. Trench	87
Just as I am	Elliott	88
Nearer Home	Carey	89
A Death-bed Hymn		90
The Sleep of Death	Hemans	92
She is not dead, but sleepeth	Hinds	92

CONTENTS.

vii

		PAGE
Heaven		93
At Home in Heaven	Montgomery	94
His servants shall serve Him	L. R.	98
And they shall see His face	Swain	100
Who shall ascend to the holy place?	Hankinson	101
The City of our God	Newton	102
Bought with a price	Doddridge	104
He had not where to lay His head	J. S. Monsell	105
The Righteous Advocate	E. Birrell	106
As many as touched were made perfectly whole	L. R.	108
Create in me a clean heart	Wesley	109
Renew a right spirit within me	Lynch	110
Lovest thou me?	Montgomery	112
Hide me under the shadow of Thy wings		112
The House of God	L. R.	113
Paraphrase on Psalm lxxxiv	H. F. Lyte	114
The Exile's Vision	Sunday at Home	116
Sabbath morning	Lyra Germanica	119
Communion with God		121
In Suffering		123
Clear Shining after Rain	Lyra Germanica	123
Songs of Praise	Montgomery	125
The Angel of Patience	M. S. M.	126
Incompleteness	A. A. Procter	127
Nearer to Thee	S. F. Adams	129
Tribulation worketh patience	Voice of Christian Life in Song	131
Clinging to Thee		132
Cast down, but not destroyed	F. F.	133
Thankfulness	A. A. Procter	134
Contentment	R. C. Trench	136
Midnight Hymn		136
Morning Hymn	Lyra Germanica	138
Pray without ceasing	L. R.	140
Thy face, Lord, will I seek	Bonar	142
Joseph, a type of Christ	C. F. Alexander	143
Glory to God in the highest	C. E.	146
An Advent Hymn	C. F. H.	147

CONTENTS.

		PAGE
When heart and flesh fail	Hemans	148
For Christ's sake	L. R.	149
Light Shining out of darkness	Cowper	151
Cowper's Grave	E. B. Browning	152
Love	L. R.	155
The Death of the Sagamore		156
The Lord is mindful of His own		161
Unto us a Son is born	Montgomery	162
Walk in the light		164
Adoration	Truman	165
God in everything	Moore	166
Freely ye have received, freely give		167
Forgiven	A. A. Procter	169
Redeemed		169
Here and there	Hymns from the Land of Luther	170
A Voice from Heaven		172
God's Acre	Longfellow	174
The Dream	S. S. Treasury	175
Sleep	F. Broderip	179
Bless us to-night		180
A Psalm of Life	Longfellow	181
The Hours	C. P. Cranch	183
Silence	T. T. Lynch	184
Open Thou our eyes	L. R.	185
Discouraged because of the way		187
When I am weak, then am I strong		188
Rock of Ages	Toplady	189
Faith in Christ		190
Looking unto Jesus	Franzén	191
Jesus	F. W.	193
A City that hath foundations		194
Sabbath		195
Quiet from God		198
Beyond	A. A. Procter	201
Living	Poems, by Author of "John Halifax"	203
For ever with the Lord	Hymns from the Land of Luther	205
Morning	Christian Year	207
Evening	Ibid	210

Christian Lyrics.

The Sleep.

"He giveth His beloved sleep."—Psalm cxxvii.

OF all the thoughts of God that are
Borne inward into souls afar,
Along the Psalmist's music deep,
Now tell me if there any is,
For gift or grace, surpassing this—
"He giveth His beloved sleep?"

What would we give to our beloved?
The hero's heart, to be unmoved,
The poet's star-tuned harp, to sweep,
The patriot's voice, to teach and rouse,
The monarch's crown, to light the brows?
"He giveth *His* beloved sleep."

What do we give to our beloved?
A little faith, all undisproved,

A little dust, to overweep,
And bitter memories, to make
The whole earth blasted for our sake.
"He giveth *His* beloved sleep."

"Sleep soft, beloved!" we sometimes say,
But have no tune to charm away
Sad dreams that through the eyelids creep:
But never doleful dream again
Shall break the happy slumber, when
"He giveth *His* beloved sleep."

O earth, so full of dreary noises!
O men, with wailing in your voices!
O delvèd gold, the wailers heap!
O strife, O curse, that o'er it fall!
God makes a silence through you all,
And "giveth His beloved sleep."

His dews drop mutely on the hill,
His cloud above it saileth still,
Though on its slope men sow and reap;
More softly than the dew is shed,
Or cloud is floated overhead,
"He giveth His beloved sleep."

Yea, men may wonder while they scan
A living, thinking, feeling man,
Confirmed, in such a rest to keep;
But angels say—and through the word,
I think their happy smile is *heard*—
"He giveth His beloved sleep."

For me, my heart that erst did go
Most like a tired child at a show,
That sees through tears the jugglers leap—
Would now its wearied vision close,
Would childlike on *His* love repose
"Who giveth His beloved sleep."

And friends, dear friends—when it shall be
That this low breath is gone from me,
And round my bier ye come to weep,
Let one, most loving of you all,
Say "Not a tear o'er her must fall—
He giveth His beloved sleep."
E. B. Browning.

The Peace of God.

WE ask for peace, O Lord!
    Thy children ask Thy peace;
Not what the world calls rest,
    That care and toil should cease,
That through bright sunny hours
    Calm life should fleet away,
And tranquil night should end
    In smiling day;—
It is not for such peace that we would pray.

We ask for peace, O Lord!
    Yet not to stand secure,

Girt round with iron pride,
   Contented to endure :
Crushing the gentle strings
   That human hearts should know,
Untouched by others' joy
     Or others' woe ;—
Thou, O dear Lord, wilt never teach us so.

We ask Thy peace, O Lord !
   Through storm, and fear, and strife,
To light and guide us on,
   Through a long struggling life :
While no success or gain
   Shall cheer the desperate fight,
Or nerve, what the world calls,
     Our wasted might :—
Yet pressing through the darkness to the light.

It is Thine own, O Lord,
   Who toil while others sleep ;
Who sow with loving care
   What other hands shall reap :
They lean on Thee entranced,
   In calm and perfect rest :
Give us that peace, O Lord,
     Divine and blest,
Thou keepest for those hearts who love Thee best.

A. A. Procter.

Prayer.

WHEN prayer delights thee least, then learn to say,
Soul, now is greatest need that thou should'st pray.

Crooked and warped I am, and I would fain
Straighten myself by thy right line again.

Oh come, warm sun, and ripen my late fruits;
Pierce, genial showers, down to my parchèd roots.

My well is bitter; cast therein the tree,
That sweet henceforth its brackish waves may be.

Say what is prayer, when it is prayer indeed?
The mighty utterance of a mighty need.

The man is praying, who doth press with might
Out of his darkness into God's own light.

White heat the iron in the furnace won,
Withdrawn from thence, 'twas cold and hard anon.

Flowers from their stalks divided, presently
Droop, fail, and wither in the gazer's eye.

The greenest leaf divided from its stem,
To speedy withering doth itself condemn.

The largest river from its fountain head
Cut off, leaves soon a parched and dusty bed.

Christian Lyrics.

All things that live from God their sustenance wait,
And sun and moon are beggars at His gate.

All skirts extended of thy mantle hold,
When angel hands from heaven are scattering gold.
R. C. Trench.

The Cloud.

A LITTLE cloud was fashioned
   In a summer hour,
By the love impassioned
   Of the sun and shower.
All day it basked in sunlight,
   On the heaven's warm blue,
Round lilies through the dun night,
   It hung in dew.

Once when dawn was leading
   In the hot young day,
This little cloud speeding
   Through the ether gray,
Seemed to float and sail
   On the bright sky's bosom,
Like a dew-drop pale
   On a blue-bell blossom.

So close under heaven
   Did it glide and fleet,
That I thought it riven
   By some angel's feet,
When the breezes parted
   Its veiling screen,
And blue glimpses darted
   Into sight between.

As I gazed came breathings
   On a zephyr's wings,
As of wild-wind wreathings
   Round Æolian strings;
'Twas a lark far hidden
   In the little cloud,
" Singing songs unbidden,"
   Full, and free, and loud.

Oh, it came down-streaming
   The clear air along,
Like rills roused from dreaming,
   Like a shower of song.
It made me glad and bright,
   Brighter every minute,
Till I blessed the cloudlet white,
   And the spirit in it.

Then the sun's noon splendour
   Filled the cloud with light,
Though a soft and tender
   Yet intensest white;

And the wanderer weary
    Joyed that it was made,
For it gave to him a cheery
    And a grateful shade.

Did the semblance of a shadow
    On the wide sky pass?
It dusked the quiet meadow,
    And the glistening grass;
It dimmed the forest fountain,
    And the clover lea;
It deepened on the mountain,
    Darkened on the sea.

Still, though earth was shaded,
    And a gloom was there,
Never dulled or faded
    Was the cloudlet fair;
For it ever sailed
    Up so close to heaven,
That nothing could have failed
    Of the beauty given.

Now a lustre glowing
    In the silent west,
From the sun was flowing
    As he turned to rest;
And the cloud borne sunward,
    Ever nearer, nigher,
Ever floated onward
    Towards the sunset fire;

All its being belted
  With a glory bright,
While into heaven it melted
  In a dream of light.
Never more glance crossed it
  In the sky-heart far,
But where I had lost it
  Shone the evening star—

Like the cloud, keep union
  With the pure and high,
Be thy communion
  Beyond the sky;
So all love and graces,
  And a light divine,
Shall have pleasant places
  In that heart of thine.

And from thee will shower,
  Upon all around,
A most precious dower,
  Like the shade and sound,
Like the music blessing
  Of lark's ziraleet,
Like the shadow's refreshing
  In the summer heat.

If trouble and sadness
  Be around, above,
Thou wilt drink deep gladness
  From thy heaven of love;

As when earth was covered
    With a twilight shroud,
Richer radiance hovered
    Round the little cloud.

And when life is ending,
    Oh, how dear to die,
Like the cloudlet, blending
    With the glorious sky!
And when unbeholden
    As its beauties are,
To have memories, golden
    As the lovely star!

                      Excelsior.

The Ivy.

THE ivy in a dungeon grew,
Unfed by rain, uncheered by dew;
Its pallid leaflets only drank
Cave moistures foul and odours dank.

But through the dungeon grating high,
There fell a sunbeam from the sky:
It slept upon the grateful floor
In silent gladness evermore.

The ivy felt a tremor shoot
Through all its fibres to the root;

It felt the light, it saw the ray,
It strove to issue into day.

It grew, it crept, it pushed, it clomb,
Long had the darkness been its home;
But well it knew, though veil'd in night,
The goodness and the joy of light.

Its clinging roots grew deep and strong;
Its stem expanded firm and long;
And in the currents of the air
Its tender branches flourished fair.

It reached the beam—it thrilled, it curled,
It blessed the warmth that cheers the world;
It rose toward the dungeon bars—
It looked upon the sun and stars.

It felt the life of bursting spring,
It heard the happy skylark sing;
It caught the breath of morns and eves,
And woo'd the swallow to its leaves.

By rains, and dews, and sunshine fed,
Over the outer wall it spread;
And in the day-beam waving free,
It grew into a steadfast tree.

Upon that solitary place
Its verdure threw adorning grace,
The mating birds became its guests,
And sang its praises from their nests.

Would'st know the moral of this rhyme?
Behold the heavenly light and climb!
Look up, O tenant of the cell,
Where man, the prisoner, must dwell.

In every dungeon comes a ray
Of God's interminable day,
On every heart a sunbeam falls,
To cheer its lonely prison walls.

The ray is Truth. Oh, soul, aspire
To bask in its celestial fire;
So shalt thou quit the glooms of clay,
So shalt thou flourish into day.

So shalt thou reach the dungeon grate,
No longer dark and desolate;
And look around thee, and above,
Upon a world of light and love.

C. Mackay.

Onward.

ONWARD! the goal thou seekest
Is worthy the quest of a life,
And love can give to the weakest
Courage and strength for the strife.

High is the prize above thee,
In the light of that golden sky;

The ladder's not all of sunshine,
Whereon thou must climb so high.

Earth's shadows and griefs have darkened,
Earth's sorrows have shaded its light,
But rays from the sunshine of heaven
Each upward step make bright.

Sometimes the glory paleth,
And its brightness disappears;
'Tis only thine eye that faileth,
Or is dimmed by earthborn tears.

Onward! our cry for ever,
Till our glorious goal be won,
'Mid the brightness fading never
Of the light-enshrouded sun.

L. R.

"Never hasting, never resting."

NEVER hasting, never resting,
   With a firm and joyous heart,
Ever onward slowly tending,
   Acting, aye, a brave man's part.

With a high and holy purpose,
   Doing all thou hast to do;
Seeking ever man's up-raising,
   With the highest end in view.

Undepressed by seeming failure,
  Unelated by success;
Heights attained revealing higher,
  Onward, upward, ever press.

Slowly moves the march of ages,
  Slowly grows the forest king,
Slowly to perfection cometh
  Every great and glorious thing.

Broadest streams from narrowest sources,
  Noblest trees from meanest seeds,
Mighty ends from small beginnings,
  From lowly promise, lofty deeds.

Acorns which the winds have scattered,
  Future navies may provide;
Thoughts at midnight whisper'd lowly,
  Prove a people's future guide.

Such the law enforced by nature
  Since the earth her course began;
Such to thee she teacheth daily,
  Eager, ardent, restless man.

" Never hasting, never resting,"
  Glad in peace, and calm in strife;
Quietly thyself preparing
  To perform thy part in life.

Earnest, hopeful, and unswerving,
  Weary though thou art, and faint,

Ne'er despair, there's One above thee,
   Listing ever to thy plaint.

Stumbleth he who runneth fast,
   Dieth he who standeth still;
Not by haste nor rest can ever
   Man his destiny fulfil.

"Never hasting, never resting,"
   Legend fine, and quaint, and olden,
In our thinking, in our acting,
   Should be writ in letters golden.

Enoch.

HAST thou not seen at break of day,
   One only star the east adorning,
That never set, or paled its ray,
But seemed to sink at once away
   Into the light of morning?

From it, the sage no portent drew,
   It came to light no meteor fires,
But silver shone the whole night through,
On hawthorn hedges steeped in dew,
   And quiet village spires.

Like him of old who dwelt beneath
   The tents of patriarchal story,
Who passed, without the touch of death,

Without dim eye or failing breath,
  At once into God's glory—

The Patriarch of one simple spot,
  The sire of sons, and daughters lowly,
And this the record of his lot,
"He walked with God and he was not,"
  For the Lord took him wholly.

Like a child's voice in sacred song,
  That trembling rises high and higher,
Till, lost at last, it peals along,
Swelling the anthem sweet and strong
  Of great cathedral choir:—

So year by year, and day by day,
  In pastoral care and household duty,
He walked with God—nor knew decay,
But faded gently, rapt away,
  Into His glorious beauty.

There's many a household fair to see,
  By woodland nook, or running river,
Where children climb the parent's knee—
Oh, that those homes like his might be,
  Filled with God's presence ever!

Oh, that our thoughts so heavenly were,
  Our hearts to Christ so fully given,
That all our loves, and toils, and care,
Might only lead us nearer there,
  Where He is set in heaven.

C. F. A.

For Ever.

THEY came, they went; of pleasures past away,
How often this is all that we can say!
They came, like dew-drops in the morning hour,
They went, like dew-drops 'neath the noontide's
    power;
Came like the cistus with its purple eye,
Went like the cistus blooming but to die;
Unheeded in their flight they glided past,
We sighed not, for we knew not 'twas the last!

There's no last time in heaven! the angels pour
A still new song, though chanted evermore,
There's no night following on their daylight hours,
No fading time for amaranthine flowers:
No change, no death, no harp that lies unstrung,
No vacant place those hallowed hills among!

Buds and Blossoms.

NOUGHT see we here as yet in full perfection,
    Nought reaching yet unto its true ideal;
Lost to our careless sight is that connection
    Which knitted once the perfect to the real.

Each form of loveliness, each fair creation,
    Hath yet a type more true and brighter far,
And we must trace in all the dim relation,
    And what they might be, learn from what they are.

Thus every character, whate'er its sweetness,
    Is but the fruit all blighted and unripe,
Still ever striving towards its own completeness,
    Still ever yearning towards its highest type.

And only as we know and love them duly,
    As buds and promise of a fairer growth,
Shall we learn how to weigh and prize them truly,
    And trace the true unto the highest truth.

Though lost and fallen is our perfect being,
    Its beauty 'mid its ruins we may see,
And strive we still, the far completeness seeing,
    To reach once more the highest we can be.

And strive we, following in our love and duty,
    Him who doth noblest, truest, purest shine,
Who raised our human to its highest beauty,
    By blending with it His own bright divine.

L. R.

The Suppliant.

ALL night the lonely suppliant prayed,
    All night his earnest crying made,
    Till, standing by his side at morn,
    The tempter said in bitter scorn,
    "O, peace : what profit do you gain,
    "From empty words and babblings vain

" 'Come, Lord—O come!' you cry alway,
" You pour your heart out night and day;
" Yet still no murmur of reply—
" No voice that answers, 'Here am I.' "

Then sank that stricken heart in dust,
That word had withered all its trust;
No strength retained it now to pray,
While faith and hope had fled away:
And ill that mourner now had fared,
Thus by the tempter's art ensnared,
But that at length beside his bed
His sorrowing angel stood, and said—
" Doth it repent thee of thy love,
" That never now is heard above
" Thy prayer; that never any more
" It knocks at heaven's gate as before?"

" I am cast out—I find no place,
" No hearing at the throne of grace;
" 'Come, Lord—O come!' I cry alway,
" I pour my heart out night and day,
" Yet never until now have won
" The answer—'Here am I, my son.' "

" Oh dull of heart—enclosed doth lie,
" In each, 'Come, Lord!' a 'Here am I,'
" Thy love, thy longing, are not thine—
" Reflections of a love divine!
" Thy very prayer to thee was given,
" Itself a messenger from heaven."

R. C. Trench.

Strive, Wait, and Pray.

STRIVE: yet I do not promise
   The prize you dream of to-day
Will not fade when you think to grasp it,
   And melt in your hand away;
But another and holier treasure,
   You would now perchance disdain,
Will come when your toil is over,
   And pay you for all your pain.

Wait; yet I do not tell you
   The hour you long for now,
Will not come with its radiance vanished,
   And a shadow upon its brow;
Yet, far through the misty future,
   With a crown of starry light,
An hour of joy you know not,
   Is winging her silent flight.

Pray; though the gift you ask for
   May never comfort your fears,
May never repay your pleading,
   Yet pray, and with hopeful tears;
An answer, not that you long for,
   But diviner, will come one day;
Your eyes are too dim to see it,
   Yet strive, and wait, and pray.

A. A. Procter.

Thou maintainest my Lot.

SOURCE of my life's refreshing springs,
   Whose presence in my heart sustains me,
Thy love appoints me pleasant things,
   Thy mercy orders all that pains me.

If loving hearts were never lonely,
   If all they wished might always be,
Accepting what they look for only,
   They might be glad, but not in Thee.

Well may Thy own beloved, who see
   In all their lot their Father's pleasure,
Bear loss of all they love, save Thee,
   Their living, everlasting treasure.

Well may Thy happy children cease
   From restless wishes prone to sin,
And in Thine own exceeding peace,
   Yield to Thy daily discipline.

We need as much the cross we bear,
   As air we breathe, as light we see;
It draws us to Thy side in prayer,
   It binds us to our strength in Thee.

                      A. L. Waring.

"Lord, and what shall this man do?"

"LORD, and what shall this man do?"
   Ask'st thou, Christian, for thy friend?
If his love for Christ be true,
   Christ hath told thee of his end:
This is he whom God approves,
This is he whom Jesus loves.

Ask not of him more than this,
   Leave it in his Saviour's breast,
Whether, early called to bliss,
   He in youth shall find his rest,
Or armèd in his station wait
Till his Lord be at the gate:

Whether in his lonely course
   (Lonely, not forlorn) he stay,
Or with Love's supporting force
   Cheat the toil and cheer the way:
Leave it all in His high hand,
Who doth hearts as streams command.

Gales from heaven, if so He will,
   Sweeter melodies can wake
On the lonely mountain rill,
   Than the meeting waters make.
Who hath the Father and the Son,
May be left, but not alone.

Sick or healthful, slave or free,
   Wealthy, or despised and poor—
What is that to him or thee,
   So his love to Christ endure?
When the shore is won at last,
Who will count the billows past?

Only, since our souls will shrink
   At the touch of natural grief,
When our earthly lov'd ones sink,
   Lend us, Lord, thy sure relief,
Patient hearts, their pain to see,
And Thy grace to follow Thee.
Christian Year.

Suspiria.

TAKE them, O Death! and bear away
   Whatever thou canst call thine own!
Thine image, stamped upon this clay,
   Doth give thee that, but that alone!

Take them, O Grave! and let them lie
   Folded upon thy narrow shelves,
As garments by the soul laid by,
   And precious only to ourselves!

Take them, O great Eternity!
   Our little life is but a gust,
That bends the branches of thy tree,
   And trails its blossoms in the dust!
Longfellow.

Mortality.

"And we shall be changed."

YE dainty mosses, lichens grey,
    Press'd each to each in tender fold,
And peacefully thus, day by day,
    Returning to their mould;—

Brown leaves, that with aërial grace
    Slip from your branch like birds a-wing,
Each leaving in the appointed place
    Its bud of future spring;—

If we, God's conscious creatures, knew
    But half your faith in our decay,
We should not tremble as we do
    When summon'd clay to clay,

But with an equal patience sweet,
    We should put off this mortal gear,
In whatsoe'er new form is meet,
    Content to re-appear.

Knowing each germ of life He gives
    Must have in Him its source and rise,
Being that of His being lives
    May change, but never dies.

Ye dead leaves, dropping soft and slow,
    Ye mosses green, and lichens fair,
Go to your graves, as I will go,
    For God is also there.

"Poems" by the Author of "John Halifax."

My Times are in Thy Hand.

FATHER, I know that all my life
  Is portioned out for me,
And the changes that are sure to come
  I do not fear to see;
But I ask Thee for a patient mind,
  Intent on pleasing Thee.

I ask Thee for a thoughtful love,
  Through constant watching wise,
To meet the glad with joyful smiles,
  And wipe the weeping eyes;
And a heart at leisure from itself,
  To soothe and sympathise.

I would not have the restless will
  That hurries to and fro,
Seeking for some great thing to do,
  . Or secret thing to know;
I would be treated as a child,
  And guided where I go.

Wherever in the world I am
  In whatsoe'er estate,
I have a fellowship with hearts
  To keep and cultivate;
And a work of lowly love to do
  For the Lord on whom I wait.

So I ask Thee for the daily strength,
   To none that ask denied,
And a mind to blend with outward life,
   While keeping at Thy side;
Content to fill a little space,
   So Thou be glorified.

And if some things I do not ask,
   In my cup of blessing be,
I would have my spirit filled the more
   With grateful love to Thee—
More careful—than to serve Thee *much*
   To please Thee perfectly.

There are briars besetting every path,
   That call for patient care;
There is a cross in every lot,
   And an earnest need for prayer;
But the lowly heart that leans on Thee;
   Is happy anywhere.

In a service that Thy love appoints,
   There are no bonds for me;
For my secret heart is taught "the truth,"
   That makes Thy children "free,"
And a life of self-renouncing love,
   Is a life of liberty.

A. L. Waring.

Milton on his Blindness.

I AM old and blind;
   Men point at me as smitten by God's frown,
Afflicted and deserted by my kind;
   Yet I am not cast down.

I am weak, yet strong;
   I murmur not that I no longer see—
Poor, old, and helpless, I the more belong,
   Father supreme! to Thee.

O merciful One!
   When men are farthest, then Thou art most near;
When friends pass by, my weakness shun,
   Thy chariot I hear.

Thy glorious face
   Is leaning towards me, and its holy light
Shines in upon my lonely dwelling place,
   And there is no more night.

On my bended knee,
   I recognise Thy purpose, clearly shown;
My vision Thou hast dimmed that I may see
   Thyself—Thyself alone.

I have nought to fear;
   This darkness is but the shadow of Thy wing:
Beneath it I am almost sacred, here
   Can come no evil thing.

Oh! I seem to stand,
   Trembling, where foot of mortal ne'er hath been,
Wrapped in the radiance of Thy sinless land,
   Which eye hath never seen.

Visions come and go;
   Shapes of resplendent beauty round me throng;
From angel lips I seem to hear the flow
   Of soft and holy song.

It is nothing now,
   When heaven is opening on my sightless eyes,
When airs from paradise refresh my brow,
   That earth in darkness lies.

In a purer clime
   My being fills with rapture—waves of thought
Roll in upon my spirit—strains sublime
   Break over me unsought.

Give me now my lyre!
   I feel the stirrings of a gift divine;
Within my bosom glows unearthly fire,
   Lit by no skill of mine.

E. Lloyd.

Trust.

COMMIT thou all thy griefs
  And ways into His hands,
To His sure truth and tender care,
  Who earth and heaven commands.

Who points the clouds their course,
  Whom winds and seas obey:
He shall direct thy wandering feet,
  He shall prepare thy way.

Put thou thy trust in God,
  In duty's path go on;
Fix on his word thy steadfast eye,
  So shall thy work be done.

No profit can'st thou gain
  By self-consuming care;
To Him commend thy cause, His ear
  Attends the softest prayer.

Give to the winds thy fears;
  Hope, and be undismayed;
God hears thy sighs, and counts thy tears;
  God shall lift up thy head.

Through waves, and clouds, and storms,
  He gently clears thy way:
Wait thou His time—thy darkest night
  Shall end in brightest day.

Gerhardt.

A Valediction.

GOD be with thee, my beloved, God be with thee!
    Else alone thou goest forth,
    Thy face unto the north—   [thee.
Moor and pleasance, all around thee and beneath
    Looking equal in one snow!
    While I who try to reach thee,
Vainly follow, vainly follow,
With the farewell and the hollo,
And cannot reach thee so.
    Alas! I can but teach thee—
God be with thee, my beloved,—God be with thee!

Can I teach thee, my beloved,—can I teach thee?
    If I said, go left or right,
    The counsel would be light,—
The wisdom poor of all that could enrich thee,
    My right would show like left;
    My raising would depress thee,—
    My choice of light would blind thee,—
    Of way, would lead behind thee,—
    Of end would leave bereft.
    Alas! I can but bless thee—
May God teach thee, my beloved,—may God teach thee!

Can I bless thee, my beloved,—can I bless thee?
    What blessing word can I
    From my own tears keep dry?
What flowers grow in my field wherewith to dress thee?

My good reverts to ill ;
My calmnesses would move thee,—
My softnesses would prick thee,—
My bindings up would break thee,—
My crownings, curse and kill.
Alas ! I can but love thee—
May God-bless thee, my beloved—may God bless thee !

Can I love thee, my beloved,—can I love thee ?
And is *this* like love, to stand
With no help in my hand,
When strong as death I fain would watch above thee ?
My love-kiss can deny
No tear that falls beneath it :
My oath of love can swear thee
From no ill that comes near thee,—
And thou diest whilst I breathe it,
And *I*,—I can but die !
May God love thee, my beloved,—may God love thee !
E. B. *Browning*.

Abide with me.

ABIDE with me ; fast falls the eventide ;
The darkness thickens : Lord, with me abide ;
When other helpers fail, and comforts flee,
Help of the helpless, O abide with me ;

Swift to its close ebbs out life's little day ;
Earth's joys grow dim, its glories pass away ;

Change and decay in all around I see:
O Thou who changest not, abide with me!

Not a brief glance I beg, a passing word,
But as Thou dwell'st with Thy disciples, Lord,—
Familiar, condescending, patient, free,
Come not to sojourn, but abide with me.

Come not in terrors, as the King of kings,
But kind and good, with healing on Thy wings;
Tears for all woes, a heart for every plea;
Come, Friend of sinners, thus abide with me.

I need Thy presence every passing hour,—
What but Thy grace can foil the tempter's power?
Who like Thyself my guide and stay can be?
Through cloud and sunshine, O abide with me!

I fear no foe, with Thee at hand to bless:
Ills have no weight, and tears no bitterness:
Where is death's sting? where, grave, thy victory?
I triumph still if Thou abide with me.

Hold Thou Thy cross before my closing eyes,
Shine through the gloom, and point me to the skies:
Heaven's morning breaks, and earth's vain shadows flee;
In life, in death, O Lord, abide with me.

H. F. Lyte.

To a Waterfowl.

WHITHER, midst falling dew,
    While glow the heavens with the last steps of
        day,
    Far through their rosy depths dost thou pursue
        Thy solitary way?

    Vainly the fowler's eye
      Might mark thy distant flight to do thee wrong,
As, darkly painted on the crimson sky,
      Thy figure floats along.

    Seek'st thou the plashy brink
Of weedy lake, or marge of river wide,
Or where the rocking billows rise or sink
      On the chafed ocean side?

    There is a power whose care
Teaches thy way along that pathless coast,—
The desert and the illimitable air,—
      Lone wandering, but not lost.

    All day thy wings have fanned,
At that far height, the cold, thin atmosphere,
Yet stoop not, weary, to the welcome land,
      Though the dark night is near.

    And soon that toil shall end;
Soon shalt thou find a summer home, and rest,
And scream among thy fellows; reeds shall bend
      Soon o'er thy sheltered nest.

Thou 'rt gone, the abyss of heaven
Hath swallowed up thy form; yet, on my heart
Deeply has sunk the lesson thou hast given,
   And shall not soon depart.

He who, from zone to zone,
Guides through the boundless sky thy certain flight,
In the long way that I must tread alone,
   Will guide my steps aright.

Bryant.

The Alpine Gentian.

SHE, 'neath ice-mountains vast
   Long had lain sleeping,
When she looked forth at last
   Timidly peeping.

Trembling she gazed around,—
   All round her slept,
O'er the dead icy ground
   Cold shadows crept.

Wide fields of silent snow,
   Still frozen seas;
What could her young life do
   'Mid such as these?

Not a voice came to her,
    Not a warm breath:
What hope lay there for her,
    Living 'midst death?

Mournfully pondering,
    Gazed she on high;
White clouds were wandering
    Through the blue sky.

There smiled the kindly sun,
    Gentle beams kissed her;
On her the mild moon shone,
    Like a saint sister.

There, twinkling, many a star
    Danced in sweet mirth;
The warm heavens seemed nearer far
    Than the cold earth.

So she gazed steadfastly
    Loving on high,
Till she grew heavenly
    Blue as the sky;

And the cold icicles
    Near her which grew,
Thawed in her skyey bells,
    Fed her with dew:

And the tired traveller
    Gazing abroad,
Fixing his eyes on her
    Thinketh of God,—

  Thinks, how 'mid life's cold snow,
   Hearts to God given,
  Breathe out, where'er they go,
   Summer and heaven.
Excelsior.

The Golden Rule.

"All things whatsoever ye would that men should do unto you, do ye even so to them."—Matt. vii, 12.

AH! not alone the murderous blade
  This golden rule would sheathe,
Not only rival states be made
  The words of peace to breathe.
But were this sacred maxim ours,
How oft life's thorns were changed to flowers,
How many a cloud that round us lowers,
  Would half its darkness lose.
Love o'er our chequered, changeful way,
Would hold its sweet yet potent sway,
Mighty as noontide's powerful ray,
  Yet soft as evening dews.

Not only near the glittering sword
  Doth war's fierce spirit dwell,
The discord of the soul, a word,
  A glance, can speak too well.
A thousand trifles, light as air
To him who can life's tempests dare,
May yet the softer spirit tear
  With wounds not deep, but keen.

And who can thus bid others smart,
Has war as surely in his heart
As he who wings the poisoned dart
    In battle's dreadful scene.

But thoughtless words may bear a sting
    Where malice hath no place,
May wake to pain some secret string
    Beyond thy power to trace.
When quivering lip, and flushing cheek,
The spirit's agony bespeak,
Then, though thou deem thy brother weak,
    Yet soothe his soul to peace.
But if the fierce and kindling eye,
Proclaim a storm of passion nigh,
Oh! then, with tenfold fervour try
    To bid the tumult cease.

For if those angry passions wake
    Within another's breast,
Thou'lt surely in his guilt partake,
    Its weight on thee will rest.
And though the crime be great in him
To let the tempest rise within,
Yet is not thine the greater sin,
    In the just view of heaven?
Whose load in many an after day,
Upon thy burdened heart may weigh,
And chase thy spirit's calm away,
    When he has been forgiven.

Perchance thy well-aimed satire draws
   A smile from those around,
But in a heartless throng's applause
   Is solid pleasure found?
Can it delight thee? surely, no;
Its brightest smiles thou would'st forego,
The fame its honours can bestow,
   Rather than wound another.
Could'st thou its worthless praise obtain,
A listening world's approval gain,
Could this atone to thee for pain
   Inflicted on a brother?

O thou, whose every nerve vibrates
   On feeling's golden chain!
Whose chords each passing breeze awakes
   To pleasure or to pain.
A living harp, whose trembling strings
Now rapture thrills, now anguish wrings,
While every whispering zephyr brings
   Some breath to swell the tone;
Remember, feelings as refined
May round thy brother's heart be twined,
And gently guard his peace of mind,
   As if it were thine own.

Thus make this sacred maxim thine,
   While life is spared to thee,
The lip that gave it was divine—
   A lip of purity.

And He whose blameless life supplied
Of holy love, a boundless tide,
Thy yielded heart would sweetly guide
    Its loveliness to see.
And were its spirit felt aright,
'Twould shed around a hallowed light,
And make this weary world as bright
    As aught 'neath heaven can be.

S. A. Storrs.

It shall be returned to thee again.

        Thy love
Shall chant itself its own beatitudes,
After its own life working. A child-kiss,
Set on thy sighing lips, shall make thee glad;
A poor man, served by thee, shall make thee rich;
A sick man, helped by thee, shall make thee strong;
Thou shalt be served thyself by every sense
Of service which thou renderest.

E. B. Browning.

Strength, Love, and Rest.

STILL evermore for some great strength we pray,
Seeking and yearning for it day by day;
A strength whereon undoubting we may lean,
And find that rest we have but dimly seen.

To lean our heart upon another heart,
In love that neither life nor death can part;
So seek we still to end our life-long quest,
For only in true love we find true rest.

That love which makes another's life our own,
And tunes our jarring natures to one tone;
The filling up of all we've sought so long;
For leaning on itself no strength is strong.

No love is perfect here, it leads us on
To love's great source—the Uncreated One;
Most true is that through which we learn to see
Most of Thy strength, and most, O Lord, of Thee.

Which sees, in all its happiness and bliss,
The promise of a joy more great than this;
Which seeks its perfectness for evermore,
In the love-light that gilds the happy shore.

O strength, O love and rest, the light that steals
From the pure sunshine of those golden fields!
Faint rays we catch e'en now upon our way,
Lighting our footsteps to the land of day.

Thou art the light, the sunshine is from Thee;
And in Thy heart is strength and purity;
There lean our weary hearts, there ends our quest,
For there is perfect love and perfect rest.

L. R.

Speak gently.

SPEAK gently!—it is better far
    To rule by love than fear;
Speak gently! let not harsh words mar
    The good we might do here!

Speak gently!—love doth whisper low
    The vows that true hearts bind;
And gently friendship's accents flow;
    Affection's voice is kind!

Speak gently to the little child,
    Its love be sure to gain;
Teach it in accents soft and mild;
    It may not long remain!

Speak gently to the young; for they
    Will have enough to bear;
Pass through this world as best they may,
    'Tis full of anxious care!

Speak gently to the aged one;
    Grieve not the careworn heart;
The sands of life are nearly run,
    Let such in peace depart.

Speak gently, kindly to the poor,
    Let no harsh tone be heard;
They have enough they must endure,
    Without an unkind word.

Speak gently to the erring! know
  They may have toiled in vain;
Perchance unkindness made them so:
  Oh! win them back again.

Speak gently! He, who gave His life
  To bend man's stubborn will,
When elements were in fierce strife,
  Said to them, "Peace, be still."

Speak gently! 'tis a little thing
  Dropped in the heart's deep well;
The good, the joy, that it may bring,
  Eternity shall tell!

Think gently of the Erring.

THINK gently of the erring;
Ye know not of the power
With which the dark temptation came,
In some unguarded hour.
Ye may not know how earnestly
They struggled, or how well,
Until the hour of weakness came,
And sadly thus they fell.

Think gently of the erring;
Oh! do not thou forget,
However darkly stained by sin,
He is thy brother yet;
Heir of the self-same heritage,
Child of the self-same God,
He has but stumbled in the path
Thou hast in weakness trod.

Speak gently to the erring;
For is it not enough
That innocence and peace have gone,
Without thy censure rough?
It sure must be a weary lot,
That sin-stained heart to bear,
And those who share a happier fate
Their chidings well may spare.

Speak gently to the erring;
Thou yet may'st lead them back
With holy words, and tones of love,
From misery's thorny track;
Forget not thou hast often sinned,
And sinful yet must be,
Deal gently with the erring then,
As God has dealt with thee.

Judge Not.

JUDGE not; the workings of his brain
   And of his heart thou can'st not see;
What looks to thy dim eyes a stain,
   In God's pure light may only be
A scar, brought from some well-won field,
Where thou would'st only faint and yield.

The look, the air, that frets thy sight,
   May be a token that below
The soul has closed in deadly fight
   With some infernal fiery foe,
Whose glance would scorch thy smiling grace,
And cast thee shuddering on thy face.

The fall thou darest to despise—
   May be the slackened angel's hand
Has suffered it, that he may rise
   And take a firmer, surer stand;
Or, trusting less to earthly things,
May henceforth learn to use his wings.

And judge none lost; but wait and see,
   With hopeful pity, not disdain;
The depth of the abyss may be
   The measure of the height of pain,
And love and glory, that may raise
This soul to God in after days.

A. A. Procter.

Faith, Hope, and Charity.

FAITH, Hope, and Charity,—these three,
Yet is the greatest—Charity;
Father of lights! these gifts impart
To mine and every human heart.

Faith, that in prayer can never fail;
Hope, that o'er doubting must prevail;
And Charity, whose name above
Is God's own name,—for God is love.

The morning star is lost in light:
Faith vanishes at perfect sight;
The rainbow passes with the storm,
And Hope with sorrow's fading form,

But Charity, serene, sublime,
Unlimited by death or time,
Like the blue sky's all-bounding space,
Holds heaven and earth in one embrace.
J. Montgomery.

Life's Lesson.

UNDER the bowering honeysuckle,
  By purple bells of shaking heather,
And brambly spines that closely buckle
  Thick-leaved chains together,
    As the sunshine plays,
    Where the lily strays

On its stream,
Netting a gauzy maze
Where the shingles gleam,
Flitting in cressy nook
Which the forget-me-not,
King-cup, and hare-bell dot,
How the glad little brook,
Sparkling along,
Singeth, in joyous measure,
Toned by its own sweet pleasure,
Music's song!

Under the night's gloom, black and starless,
When the old forest-beeches near its
Darkling flood, like trees are far less
Than like shadowy spirits;
Though the sunlight's gone
That so sweetly shone,
And the flowers
Died, as the night came on,
With the golden hours;
Though the blossom and beam,
Though the love and the light
From the glamour of night,
Have deserted its stream,
How the lone rill,
Chilled and forsaken—listen!—
Makes, though no starlight glisten,
Music still!

Excelsior.

The Streamlet's Song.

A LITTLE brook went singing,
    All through the summer hours,
Ever a low soft murmur
    It whispered to the flowers.
The bulrush and the sedgegrass
    Its leafy border made,
And the low-bending willow
    Gave cool and quiet shade.

The young birds loved its shelter,
    And listened to its song,
They tried to learn its cadence
    As it carolled it along.
What was the brooklet singing,
    What did its murmur say,
Its dreamy tones of music
    Through all the summer day?

A child came to its margin,
    It sang its song to her:
"Fair child," it said, "I'm joyous
    " As spring-time's flowerets are.
" For life is glad and sunny,
    "And who so gay as I?
" For flowerets kiss me as I pass
    " Beneath the glowing sky."

A maiden watched the brooklet,
    To her its low voice said,
" Calm my life has always been
    " In this fair meadow led.
" If clouds have dimmed the brightness,
    " They quickly passed away,
" And when I have reached the river,
    " I shall be always gay."

Long years had changed the maiden,
    When there she stood again;
Youth's glee had left her spirit,
    Her eyes were dim with pain.
Was it the song her childhood,
    Or that her girlhood knew,
That reached her world-worn spirit
    Watching its waters blue?

She heard a sadder murmur
    Than she had heard before:
" Oh never gleams the sunlight
    " In brightness as of yore.
" I'm weary of the meadow,
    " I'm weary of my tune,
" The nights are dark and cheerless,
    " The winter cometh soon."

An aged woman watched it
    With tear-dimmed anxious eye,
And bent her ear to listen
    To the streamlet's symphony.

But oh, it sang that evening
  A changed, a sadder sound :
" I go my weary journey,
  " To that great ocean bound.

" My life is sad and restless,
  " I water many a grave,
" I fear the heaving ocean,
  " I fear the mighty wave,"—
But still the child and maiden,
  And weary woman's heart,
Read not aright its lesson,
  Nor what its music taught.

Their own hearts beat too loudly
  The stream's low tones to hear,
Their spirits' voices heard they
  And not its music clear.
I'll tell you what it murmured,
  What were the words it sung,
As blue-bells kissed its waters,
  And sedgegrass o'er it hung.

It said, " My life is humble,
  " But very tranquil too,
" I gaze for ever upwards
  " On that deep sky of blue.
" After the cloudlets gather,
  " The sunshine seems more bright,
" I know the morning cometh,
  " Though dark may be the night.

" Sometimes the flowerets wither,
    " I make them fresh again,
" I bathe the thirsty willows
    " When falls no gentle rain.
" The work my Maker gives me
    " It makes me glad to do,
" His smile is in the sunshine,
    " His blessing in the dew.

" The ocean I am nearing
    " Is beautiful and fair;
" He leads me through the meadow,
    " He'll make me happy there.
" And anywhere and everywhere,
    " So that I do His will,
" And do my life's work bravely
    " I shall be happy still."

L. R.

Hymn of the City.

NOT in the solitude
    Alone may man commune with heaven, or see
Only in savage wood
    And sunny vale, the present Deity;
Or only hear His voice
Where the winds whisper and the waves rejoice.

Even here do I behold
   Thy steps, Almighty!—here amidst the crowd,
Through the vast city rolled,
   With everlasting murmur deep and loud—
Choking the ways that wind
'Mongst the proud piles, the work of human kind.

Thy golden sunshine comes
   From the round heaven, and on their dwelling lies,
And lights their inner homes:
   For them Thou fill'st with air the unbounded skies,
And givest them the stores
Of ocean, and the harvest of its shores.

Thy spirit is around,
   Quickening the restless mass that sweeps along;
And this eternal sound—
   Voices and footfalls of the numberless throng,
Like the resounding sea,
Or like the rainy tempest, speaks of Thee.

And when the hours of rest
   Come, like a calm upon the mid-sea brine,
Hushing its billowy breast—
   The quiet of that moment too is Thine,
It breathes of Him who keeps
The vast and helpless city while it sleeps.

                                Bryant.

Omnipresence.

FATHER and Friend! Thy light, Thy love
Beaming through all Thy works we see;
Thy glory gilds the heavens above,
And all the earth is full of Thee.

Thy voice we hear, Thy presence feel,
Whilst Thou, too pure for mortal sight,
Involved in clouds—invisible,
Reignest the Lord of life and light.

We know not in what hallowed part
Of the wide heavens Thy throne may be,
But this we know, that where Thou art,
Strength, wisdom, goodness, dwell with Thee.

Thy children shall not faint or fear,
Sustained by this delightful thought,
Since Thou their God art everywhere,
They cannot be where Thou art not.
Bowring.

The Brooklet.

" SWEET brooklet, ever gliding,
" Now high the mountain riding,
" The low vale now dividing,
            " Whither away?"

" With pilgrim course I flow ;
" Or in summer's scorching glow,
" Or in moonless waste of snow,
   " Nor stop nor stay:
" For oh, by high behest,
" To a home of glorious rest,
" In my parent ocean's breast,
   " I haste away."

" Many a dark morass,
" Many a craggy mass,
" Thy feeble force must pass,
   " Yet, yet delay !"
" Though the marsh be dire and deep,
" Though the crag be stern and steep,
" On, on, my course must keep,
   " I may not stay.
" For oh ! be it east or west,
" To a home of glorious rest,
" In the bright sea's boundless breast,
   " I haste away."

" The warbling bowers beside thee,
" The laughing flowers that hide thee,
" With soft accord they chide thee,
   " Sweet brooklet, stay !"
" I taste of the fragrant flowers,
" I respond to the warbling bowers,
" Sweetly they charm the hours
   " On my winding way.

"But ceaseless still, in quest
"Of that eternal rest
"In my parent's boundless breast,
   "I haste away!"

"Knowest thou the drear abyss?
"Is it a scene of bliss?
"Oh! rather cling to this;
   "Sweet brooklet, stay!"

"Oh! who shall fitly tell
"What wonders there may dwell;
"That world of mystery well
   "Might strike dismay!

"But I know 'tis my parent's breast;
"There held, I must needs be blest;
"And with joy to my promised rest
   "I haste away!"

     Sir R. Grant.

A Morning Prayer.

THE golden morn flames up the eastern sky,
And what dark night had hid from every eye
 All-piercing day-light summons clear to view:
And all the forests, vale, or plain, or hill,
That slept in mist enshrouded, dark and still,
 In gladsome light are glittering now anew.

Shine in my heart, and bring me joy and light,
Sun of my darken'd soul, dispel its night,
   And shed in it the truthful day abroad ;
And all the many gloomy folds lay bare
Within this heart, that fain would learn to wear
   The pure and glorious likeness of its Lord.

Glad with Thy light, and glowing with Thy love,
So let me ever think, and speak, and move,
   As fits a soul new-touch'd with life from heaven,
That seeks but so to order all her course,
As most to shew the glory of that source
   By whom alone her strength, her life are given.

I ask not, take away this weight of care ;
No, for that love I pray that all can bear,
   And for the faith that whatsoe'er befall
Must needs be good, and for my profit prove,
Since from my Father's heart, most rich in love,
   And from His bounteous hands it cometh all.

I ask not that my course be calm and still ;
No, here too, Lord, be done Thy holy will ;
   I ask but for a quiet, child-like heart ;
Though thronging cares and restless toil be mine,
Yet may my heart remain for ever Thine,
   Draw it from earth, and fix it were Thou art.

I ask Thee not to finish soon the strife,
The toil, the trouble of this earthly life ;
   No, be my peace amid its grief and pain ;

I pray not, grant me *now* Thy realm on high;
No, ere I die let me to evil die,
   And through Thy cross my sins be wholly slain.

True Morning Sun of all my life, I pray
That not in vain Thou shine on me to-day,
   Be Thou my light when all around is gloom;
Thy brightness, hope, and courage on me shed,
That I may joy to see, when life is fled,
   The setting sun that brings the pilgrim home.
Lyra Germanica.

The Second Day.

"And God said, let there be a firmament.

  THIS world I deem
  But a beautiful dream
  Of shadows that are not what they seem;
  Where visions arise,
  Giving dim surmise
  Of the sights that shall meet our waking eyes.

  Arm of the Lord!
  Creating Word;
  Whose glory the silent skies record,
  Where stands Thy name
  In scrolls of flame,
  On the firmament's high-shadowing frame!

I gaze o'erhead,
Where Thy hand hath spread
For the waters of heaven, their crystal bed;
And stored the dew
In its depths of blue,
Which the fires of the sun come tempered through.

Soft they shine
Through that pure shrine,
As beneath the veil of Thy flesh divine
Beams forth the light,
That were else too bright
For the feebleness of a sinner's sight.

And such I deem
This world will seem
When we waken from life's uncertain dream,
And burst the shell
Where our spirits dwell
In this wondrous ante-natal cell.

I gaze aloof
At the tissued roof,
Where time and space are the warp and woof,
Which the King of kings
As a curtain flings
O'er the dreadfulness of eternal things.

As a tapestried tent,
To shade us meant,
From the bare everlasting firmament;

Where the blaze of the skies
Comes soft to our eyes,
Through a veil of mystical imageries.

But could I see
As in truth they be,
The glories of heaven that encompass me,
I should lightly hold
The tissued fold
Of this marvellous curtain of blue and gold.

And soon the whole,
As a parched scroll,
Shall to my amazed sight uproll;
And without a screen
At one burst be seen,
The presence in which I have ever been.

Oh! who shall bear
The blinding glare
Of the majesty that shall meet us there?
What eye can gaze
On the unveiled blaze
On the light-gilded throne of the Ancient of days?

Christ us aid!
Himself be our shade,
That in that dread day we be not dismayed.
Whytehead.

The Bright and Morning Star.

THE last sand from time's hour-glass
    Shall soon disappear,
And like vapour shall vanish
    This old rolling sphere.

On the floor like the chaff-stream
    In the dark wintry day,
From the fan of destruction
    Shall suns drift away.

And the meteors of glory
    Which wilder the wise,
Only gleam till we open
    In true worlds our eyes.

But aloft in God's heaven
    There blazeth a star,
And I live while I'm watching
    Its light from afar.

From its lustre immortal
    My soul caught the spark,
Which shall beam on undying,
    When sunshine is dark.

So transforming its radiance,
    Its strength so benign,
Dull clay burns a ruby,
    And man grows divine.

To the zenith ascended,
    From Joseph's dark tomb,
Star of Jesse; so rivet
    My gaze through the gloom,

That, Thy beauty imbibing,
    My dross may refine,
Till in splendour reflected
    I burn and I shine.

Heavenward.

HEAVENWARD doth our journey tend,
    We are strangers here on earth,
Through the wilderness we wend
    Towards the Canaan of our birth.
Here we roam a pilgrim band,
Yonder is our native land.

Heavenward stretch, my soul, thy wings,
    Heavenly nature canst thou claim,
There is nought of earthly things
    Worthy to be all thine aim;
Every soul that God inspires,
Back to Him, its source, aspires.

Heavenward! doth His spirit cry,
    When I hear Him in His word

Showing thus the rest on high,
    Where I shall be with my Lord.
When His word fills all my thought,
Oft to heaven my soul is caught.

Heavenward ever would I haste,
    When thy table, Lord, is spread;
Heavenly strength on earth I taste,
    Feeding on the Living Bread;
Such is e'en on earth our fare
Who Thy marriage feast shall share.

Heavenward! faith discerns the prize,
    That is waiting us afar,
And my heart would swiftly rise,
    High o'er sun and moon and star,
To that light behind the veil
Where all earthly splendours pale.

Heavenward death shall lead at last,
    To the home where I would be,
All my sorrows overpast,
    I shall triumph there with Thee,
Jesus who hast gone before,
That we too might heavenward soar.

Heavenward! heavenward! only this
    Is my watchword on the earth;
For the love of heavenly bliss
    Counting all things little worth.
Heavenward all my being tends
Till in heaven my journey ends.
                  Lyra Germanica.

The Building of the House.

I HAVE a wondrous house to build,
    A dwelling, humble yet divine;
A lowly cottage to be filled
    With all the jewels of the mine.
How shall I build it strong and fair,
This noble house, this lodging rare,
    So small and modest, yet so great?
How shall I fill its chambers bare,
    With use, with ornament, with state?

My God hath given the stone and clay,
    'Tis I must fashion them aright;
'Tis I must mould them day by day,
    And make my labour my delight;
This cot, this palace, this fair home,
This pleasure house, this holy dome,
    Must be in all proportions fit,
That heavenly messengers may come
    To lodge with him who tenants it.

No fairy bower this house must be,
    To totter at each gale that starts,
But of substantial masonry,
    Symmetrical in all its parts;
Fit in its strength to stand sublime
For seventy years of mortal time,
    Defiant of the storm and rain,

And well attemper'd to the clime,
　　In every cranny, nook, and pane.

I'll build it so, that if the blast
　　Around it whistle loud and long,
The tempest, when its rage has pass'd,
　　Shall leave its rafters doubly strong.
I'll build it so that travellers by
Shall view it with admiring eye,
　　For its commodiousness and grace:
Firm on the ground—straight to the sky,
　　A meek but goodly dwelling place.

Thus noble in its outward form,
　　Within I'll build it clean and white,
Not cheerless cold, but happy warm,
　　And ever open to the light.
No tortuous passages or stair,
No chamber foul, or dungeon lair,
　　No gloomy attic shall there be,
But wide apartments ordered fair,
　　And redolent of purity.

With three compartments furnished well,
　　The house shall be a home complete;
Wherein, should circumstance rebel,
　　The humble tenant may retreat.
The first a room wherein to deal
With men for human nature's weal,
　　A room where he may work or play,
And all his social life reveal
　　In its pure texture day by day.

The second, for his wisdom sought,
  Where, with his chosen book or friend,
He may employ his active thought
  To virtuous and exalted end.
A chamber lofty and serene,
With a door-window to the green
  Smooth-shaven sward, and arching bowers,
Where lore or talk, or song between,
  May gild his intellectual hours.

The third an oratory dim,
  But beautiful; where he may raise,
Unheard of men, his daily hymn
  Of love and gratitude and praise.
Where he may revel in the light
Of things unseen and infinite,
  And learn how little he may be,
And yet how awful in thy sight,
  Ineffable eternity.

Such is the house that I must build,
  This is the cottage—this the dome—
And this the palace, treasure filled
  For an immortal's earthly home.
Oh noble work of toil and care!
Oh task most difficult and rare!
  Oh simple but most arduous plan!
To raise a dwelling place so fair—
  The sanctuary of a man.

C. Mackay.

"How old art thou?"

COUNT not the days that have idly flown,
    The years that were vainly spent;
Nor speak of the hours thou must blush to own,
When thy spirit stands before the throne,
    To account for the talents lent.

But number the hours redeemed from sin,
    The moments employed for heaven;
Oh! few and evil thy days have been,
Thy life, a toilsome but worthless scene,
    For a nobler purpose given.

Will the shade go back on thy dial-plate?
    Will thy sun stand still on his way?
Both hasten on; and thy spirit's fate
Rests on the point of life's little date:
    Then live while 'tis called to-day.

Life's waning hours, like the Sybil's page,
    As they lessen, in value rise:
Oh! rouse thee and live! nor deem man's age
Stands in the length of his pilgrimage,
    But in days that are truly wise.

Thy way, not mine.

THY way, not mine, O Lord,
   However dark it be!
Lead me by Thine own hand,
   Choose out the path for me.

Smooth let it be or rough,
   It will be still the best,
Winding or straight it leads
   Right onward to Thy rest.

I dare not choose my lot:
   I would not, if I might;
Choose Thou for me, my God,
   So shall I walk aright.

The kingdom that I seek
   Is Thine; so let the way
That leads to it be Thine,
   Else I must surely stray.

Take Thou my cup, and it
   With joy or sorrow fill
As best to Thee may seem;
   Choose Thou my good and ill.

Choose Thou for me my friends,
   My sickness or my health;
Choose Thou my cares for me,
   My poverty or wealth.

Not mine, not mine the choice,
　In things or great or small;
Be Thou my guide, my strength,
　My wisdom, and my all.

Bonar.

Resignation.

FATHER! whate'er of earthly bliss
　Thy sovereign will denies,
Accepted at Thy throne of grace,
　Let this petition rise:

"Give me a calm, a thankful heart,
　"From every murmur free:
"The blessings of Thy grace impart,
　"And make me live to Thee.

"Let the sweet hope that Thou art mine
　"My life and death attend;
"Thy presence through my journey shine,
　"And crown my journey's end!"

Steele.

Commit Thy way to God.

COMMIT thy way to God,
    The weight which makes thee faint;
Worlds are to Him no load,
    To Him breathe thy complaint.
He who for winds and clouds
    Maketh a pathway free,
Through wastes, or hostile crowds,
    Can make a way for thee.

Thou must in Him be blest,
    Ere bliss can be secure;
On His work must thou rest
    If thy work shall endure.
To anxious, prying thought,
    And weary, fretting care,
The Highest yieldeth nought;
    He giveth all to prayer!

Father! Thy faithful love,
    Thy mercy, wise and mild,
Sees what will blessing prove,
    Or what will hurt Thy child.
And what Thy wise foreseeing,
    Doth for Thy children choose,
Thou bringest into being,
    Nor suff'rest them to lose.

All means always possessing,
    Invincible in might ;
Thy doings are all blessing,
    Thy goings are all light.
Nothing Thy work suspending,
    No foe can make Thee pause,
When Thou, Thine own defending,
    Dost undertake their cause.

Hope then, though woes be doubled,
    Hope and be undismayed ;
Let not thine heart be troubled,
    Nor let it be afraid.
This prison where thou art,
    Thy God will break it soon,
And flood with light thy heart
    In His own blessed noon.

Up, up ! the day is breaking,
    Say to thy cares, good night !
Thy troubles from thee shaking,
    Like dreams in day's fresh light.
Thou wearest not the crown,
    Nor the best course canst tell ;
God sitteth on the throne,
    And guideth all things well.

Trust Him to govern, then !
    No king can rule like Him ;
How wilt thou wonder when
    Thine eyes no more are dim ;

To see those paths which vex thee,
  How wise they were and meet;
The works which now perplex thee,
  How beautiful, complete!

Faithful the love thou sharest,
  All, all is well with thee;
The crown from hence thou bearest
  With shouts of victory.
In thy right hand to-morrow,
  Thy God shall place the palms;
To Him who chased thy sorrow
  How glad will be thy psalms.
            Paul Gerhardt.

He doeth all things well.

I HOPED that with the brave and strong
  My portioned task might lie;
To toil amid the busy throng
  With purpose pure and high:
But God has fixed another part,
  And He has fixed it well;
I said so with my breaking heart,
  When first this anguish fell.

These weary hours will not be lost,
  These days of misery,
These nights of darkness, tempest-tost,—
  Can I but turn to Thee;

With secret labour to sustain
  In patience every blow,
To gather fortitude from pain,
  And holiness from woe.

If Thou shouldst bring me back to life,
  More humble I should be,
More wise, more strengthened for the strife,
  More apt to lean on Thee;
Should death be standing at the gate,
  Thus should I keep my vow;
But, Lord! whatever be my fate,
  Oh, let me serve Thee now!

Anne Brontë.

Love to God.

WE love Thee, Lord, yet not alone
  Because Thy bounteous hand
Showers down its rich and ceaseless gifts
  On ocean and on land:
Because Thou bidst the Sun go forth
  Rejoicing in his might,
And kindle earth to glowing life
  And beauty with his light.

Because Thou roll'st the orbs of light
  Through trackless fields of space,
And giv'st to each low creeping flower
  Its fragrance and its grace:

Because in sunshine and in storm
    Alike we see Thee near;
In summer gale and rushing wind,
    Alike Thy voice we hear:

'Tis not alone because Thy names
    Of Wisdom, Power, and Love,
Are written on the earth beneath,
    The glorious skies above.
For these Thy gifts we praise Thee, Lord;
    Yet not for these alone,
The incense of Thy children's love
    Arises to Thy throne.

We love Thee, Lord, because, when we
    Had erred and gone astray,
Thou didst recall our wandering souls
    Into the heavenward way;
When helpless, hopeless, we were lost
    In sin and sorrow's night,
Thou didst send forth a guiding ray
    Of Thy benignant light.

Because, when we forsook Thy ways,
    Nor kept Thy holy will,
Thou wert not the avenging Judge,
    But gracious Father still;
Because we have forgot Thee, Lord,
    Yet Thou hast not forgot;
Because we have forsaken Thee,
    Yet Thou forsakest not:—

Because, O Lord, Thou lovedst us
   With everlasting love:
Because Thy Son came down to die,
   That we might live above;
Because, when we were heirs of wrath,
   Thou gavest hopes of heaven:
Yes; much we love, who much have sinned,
   And much have been forgiven.

I. A. E.

Undertake for me.

AS those that watch for the day,
   Through the restless night of pain
When the first faint streaks of grey
   Bring rest and ease again—
As they turn their sleepless eyes
   The eastern sky to see,
Long hours before sunrise—
   So waiteth my soul for Thee!

As those that watch for the day,
   Through the long, long night of grief,
When the soul can only pray
   That the day may bring relief,—
When the eyes with weeping spent,
   No dawn of hope can see,
But the heart keeps watch intent,—
   So waiteth my soul for Thee!

As those that watch for the day,
   Through that deepest night of all,
When trembling and sin have sway,
   And the shades of Thy absence fall:
As they search through clouds of fear
   The Morning Star to see,
And the Light of Life appear—
   So waiteth my soul for Thee!

As those that watch for the day,
   And know that the day will rise,
Though the weary hours delay,
   As they pass under midnight skies,
Though the sun of righteousness
   Only faith's eye can see,
Because Thou hast promised to bless,
   Lord Jesus, I wait for Thee.

The Promised One.

FROM "DAVID PLAYING BEFORE SAUL."

SEE! the dull dense clouds are breaking,
   Slowly, slowly into light away!
And my mental sense is waking,
   Dazzled by a brighter ray
Than e'er, the east with glory streaking,
   Glanced from the opening eyes of day.

Is it come?—that glimpse of heaven,
For which my soul so long hath striven,
Diving for lore obscure and high,
In the darkling depths of prophecy?
Avaunt thee, fiend! the woman's seed shall tread
On the fierce terrors of the serpent's head.

I know Him by the light He giveth;
I know that my Redeemer liveth:
He shall stand upon the earth,
Godlike in His mortal birth;
In Him the sons of sorrow shall find rest,
And all the nations of the world be blest.

Yes, I know Him from afar,—
Israel's sceptre,—Jacob's star;
For, like him on Zophin's brow,
   Him of the gifted eye,
I shall see Him, but not now,
   Behold Him, but not nigh.

Be it so! on other eyes
Let the promised One arise,
While mine own are curtained deep,
In their last and soundest sleep:
Enough for me, what hope sublime
Can to her humble child allow;
Enough!—anticipating time,
She feels Him and adores Him now.

Hankinson.

Christmas Day.

WHAT sudden blaze of song
    Spreads o'er th' expanse of heav'n?
In waves of light it thrills along,
    Th' angelic signal given—
"Glory to God!" from yonder central fire
Flows out the echoing lay beyond the starry quire;

Like circles widening round
    Upon a clear blue river,
Orb after orb, the wondrous sound
    Is echoed on for ever:
"Glory to God on high, on earth be peace,
"And love towards men of love—salvation and release."

Yet stay, before thou dare
    To join that festal throng;
Listen and mark what gentle air
    First stirr'd the tide of song;
'Tis not "the Saviour born in David's home
"To whom for power and health obedient worlds
    "should come:"—

'Tis not, "the Christ the Lord:"
    With fix'd adoring look
The choir of angels caught the word,
    Nor yet their silence broke:
But when they heard the sign, where Christ
    should be,
In sudden light they shone and heavenly harmony.

Wrapped in His swaddling bands,
And in His manger laid,
The hope and glory of all lands
Is come to the world's aid:
No peaceful home upon His cradle smiled,
Guests rudely went and came, where slept the royal Child.

But where Thou dwellest, Lord,
No other thought should be,
Once duly welcom'd and ador'd,
How should I part with Thee?
Bethlehem must lose Thee soon, but Thou wilt grace
The single heart to be Thy sure abiding-place.

Thee, on the bosom laid
Of a pure virgin mind,
In quiet ever, and in shade,
Shepherd and sage may find;
They who had bow'd untaught to nature's sway,
And they who follow truth along her star-paved way.

The pastoral spirits first
Approach Thee, Babe divine,
For they in lowly thoughts are nurs'd,
Meet for Thy lowly shrine;
Sooner than they should miss where Thou dost dwell
Angels from heaven will stoop to guide them to Thy cell.

Still, as the day comes round
For Thee to be reveal'd,
By wakeful shepherds Thou art found,
Abiding in the field.
All through the wintry heaven and chill night air
In music and in light Thou dawnest on their prayer.

Oh faint not ye for fear—
What though your wandering sheep,
Reckless of what they see and hear,
Lie lost in wilful sleep?
High heaven, in mercy to your sad annoy,
Still greets you with glad tidings of immortal joy.

Think on the eternal home,
The Saviour left for you;
Think on the Lord most holy, come
To dwell with hearts untrue:
So shall ye tread untir'd His pastoral ways,
And in the darkness sing your carol of high praise.
Christian Year.

A Christmas Carol.

IT came upon the midnight clear
That glorious song of old,
From angels bending near the earth
To touch their harps of gold:

" Peace on the earth—good will to men
  " From heaven's all-gracious King;"
The world in solemn stillness lay
  To hear the angels sing.

Still through the cloven skies they come,
  With peaceful wings unfurl'd
And still their heavenly music floats
  O'er all the weary world.
Above its sad and lowly plains
  They bend on heavenly wing,
And ever o'er its Babel sounds
  The blessed angels sing.

Yet with the woes of sin and strife
  The world has suffered long,
Beneath the angel-strain have rolled
  Two thousand years of wrong;
And man, at war with man, hears not
  The love-song which they bring,—
Oh hush the noise, ye men of strife,
  And hear the angels sing!

And ye, beneath life's crushing load
  Whose forms are bending low,
Who toil along the climbing way,
  With painful steps and slow;
Look now! for glad and golden hours
  Come swiftly on thy wing—
O rest beside the weary road
  And hear the angels sing!

For lo ! the days are hastening on,
  By prophet-bards foretold,
When with the ever-circling years
  Comes round the age of gold ;
When peace shall over all the earth
  Its ancient splendours fling,
And the whole world send back the song
  Which now the angels sing.

E. H. Sears.

Robins and their Songs.

ROBIN, to the bare bough clinging,
  What can thy blithe music mean?
Like a hidden fount, thy singing
  Seems to clothe the trees with green.

What warm nest for thee hath nature,
  Where thy soft red breast to lay?
Sing'st thou, little homeless creature,
  For the crumbs we strewed to-day?

Other birds have fled this dun light,
  Soaring on to regions fair,
Singing in the richest sunlight,
  Singing in the starlit air ;

Hiding 'mid the broad-leaved shadows
  Of the southern woods at noon,
Filling all the flower-starred meadows
  With the melodies of June.

Knowest thou the woods have voices,
  Poet-voices, full and clear ;—
Strains at which the heart rejoices,
  Feeling the unspoken near ;

Pouring music like a river,
  Many-toned and deep and strong,
Tones 'midst which, like childhood's, quiver
  Thy few notes of simple song ?

Then the "crimson-tipped" thing,
  Like a daisy among birds,
With a quiet glee, did sing
  Strains condensèd thus in words :

" Well I know the joyous mazes
  " Of the songs so full and fine :—
" Very faint would be God's praises,
  " Sounded by no voice but mine !

" Yet the little child's sweet laughter,
  " Wakes it no responsive smile,
" Though the poet singeth after,
  " And the angels all the while ?

" What I sing I cannot measure,
  " Why I sing I cannot say,
" But I know a well of pleasure
  " Springeth in my heart all day."

So I learned that crumbs are able
  Lowly hearts to fill with song—
Crumbs from off that festal table
  Lowly hearts will join ere long.

He who wintry hours hath given,
  With the snows gives snow-drops birth;
And while angels sing in heaven,
  God hears robins sing on earth.

Only keep thee on the wing,
  Music dieth in the dust,
Nothing that but creeps can sing,
  Soaring, we can sing and trust.

Excelsior.

Make Thy face to shine upon Thy servant.

CHRIST, whose glory fills the skies,
  Christ, the true, the only light,
Sun of righteousness, arise,
  Triumph o'er the shades of night;
Day spring from on high, be near,
Day star, in my heart appear.

Dark and cheerless is the morn,
  Unaccompanied by Thee;
Joyless is the day's return,
  Till Thy mercy's beams I see,
Till they inward life impart,
  Glad my eyes and warm my heart.

Visit then this soul of mine,
   Pierce the gloom of sin and grief,
Fill me, radiancy divine,
   Scatter all my unbelief;
More and more Thyself display,
   Shining to the perfect day.

"Lord, that I might receive my sight."

LORD! we sit and cry to Thee
   Like the blind beside the way:
Make our darken'd souls to see
   The glory of Thy perfect day!
Lord, rebuke our sullen night,
And give Thyself unto our sight!

Lord! we do not ask to gaze
   On our dim and earthly sun;
But the light that still shall blaze
   When every star its course hath run,
The light that gilds Thy blest abode,
The glory of the Lamb of God.

Milman.

Looking unto Jesus.

THOU, who didst stoop below
  To drain the cup of woe,
Wearing the form of frail mortality—
  Thy blessed labours done,
  Thy crown of victory won,
Hast passed from earth—passed to Thy home on high.

  Man may no longer trace,
  In Thy celestial face,
The image of the bright, the viewless One;
  Nor may Thy servants hear,
  Save with faith's raptured ear,
Thy voice of tenderness, God's holy Son!

  Our eyes behold Thee not,
  Yet hast Thou not forgot
Those who have placed their hope, their trust in Thee;
  Before Thy Father's face
  Thou hast prepared a place,
That where Thou art, there they may also be.

  It was no path of flowers,
  Through this dark world of ours,
Beloved of the Father, Thou didst tread;
  And shall we in dismay,
  Shrink from the narrow way,
When clouds and darkness are around it spread?

O Thou who art our life,
Be with us through the strife!
Was not Thy head by earth's fierce tempests
    bowed?
Raise Thou our eyes above
To see a Father's love
Beam, like the bow of promise, through the
    cloud.

E'en through the awful gloom,
Which hovers o'er the tomb,
That light of love our guiding star shall be;
Our spirits shall not dread
The shadowy way to tread,
Friend, Guardian, Saviour, which doth lead to
    Thee.
Christian Examiner.

Cast me not away from Thy presence.

FORTH from the dark and stormy sky,
Lord, to Thine altar's shade we fly;
Forth from the world, its hope and fear,
Saviour, we seek Thy shelter here:
Weary and weak, Thy grace we pray;
Turn not, O Lord, Thy guests away!

Long have we roamed in want and pain,
Long have we sought Thy rest in vain;
Wildered in doubt, in darkness lost,
Long have our souls been tempest tost:
Low at Thy feet our sins we lay;
Turn not, O Lord, Thy guests away!

Heber.

"Pray without ceasing."

Go when the morning shineth,
   Go when the moon is bright,
Go when the eve declineth,
   Go in the hush of night:
Go with pure mind and feeling,
   Fling earthly thoughts away,
And in thy chamber kneeling,
   Do thou in secret pray.

Remember all who love thee,
   All who are loved by thee;
Pray too for those who hate thee,
   If any such there be:
Then for thyself in meekness
   A blessing humbly claim,
And link with each petition
   Thy great Redeemer's name.

But if 'tis e'er denied thee
  In solitude to pray,—
Should holy thoughts come o'er thee
  When friends are round thy way;
E'en then the silent breathing,
  Of thy spirit raised above,
Shall reach His throne of glory,
  Who is mercy, truth, and love.

Oh, not a joy or blessing
  With this can we compare,
The power that He hath given us
  To pour our souls in prayer.
Whene'er thou pin'st in sadness,
  Before His footstool fall:
Remember in thy gladness
  His love who gave thee all.

Lord Morpeth.

Let us Pray.

LORD, what a change within us one short hour
Spent in Thy presence will avail to make;
What burdens lighten, what temptations slake,
What parchèd grounds refresh as with a shower.
We kneel, and all around us seems to lower;
We rise, and all, the distant and the near,
Stands forth in sunny outline, brave and clear;

We kneel how weak, we rise how full of power:
Why therefore should we do ourselves this wrong,
Or others—that we are not always strong,
That we are ever overborne with care,
That we should ever weak or heartless be,
Anxious or troubled, when with us is prayer,
And joy, and strength, and courage, are with Thee.
R. C. Trench

Just as I am.

JUST as I am—without one plea,
But that Thy blood was shed for me,
And that Thou bid'st me come to Thee—
   O Lamb of God, I come.

Just as I am—and waiting not
To rid my soul of one dark blot;
To Thee whose blood can cleanse each spot—
   O Lamb of God, I come.

Just as I am—though tossed about
With many a conflict, many a doubt,
Fightings within, and fears without—
   O Lamb of God, I come.

Just as I am—poor, wretched, blind;
Sight, riches, healing of the mind,
Yea all I need, in Thee to find—
   O Lamb of God, I come.

Just as I am—Thou wilt receive,
Wilt welcome, pardon, cleanse, relieve:
Because Thy promise I believe—
  O Lamb of God, I come.

Just as I am—Thy love unknown
Has broken every barrier down;
Now to be Thine, yea, Thine alone—
  O Lamb of God, I come.

Elliott.

Nearer Home.

ONE sweetly solemn thought
    Comes to me o'er and o'er—
I'm nearer home to-day,
    Than I ever have been before.

Nearer my Father's house,
    Where the many mansions be;
Nearer the great white throne;
    Nearer the crystal sea—

Nearer the bound of life,
    Where we lay our burdens down;
Nearer leaving the cross;
    Nearer gaining the crown.

But lying darkly between,
   Winding down through the night,
Is the dim and unknown stream
   That leads at last to the light.

Closer, closer, my feet,
   Come to that dark abysm;
Closer, death to my lips
   Presses the awful chrysm.

Saviour, perfect my trust,
   Strengthen the might of my faith;
Let me feel as I would when I stand
   On the rock of the shore of death.

Feel as I would when my feet
   Are slipping over the brink;
For it may be, I'm nearer home,
   Nearer now than I think.

Carey.

A Death-Bed Hymn.

"We would see Jesus"—for the shadows lengthen
   Across this little landscape of our life;
"We would see Jesus," our weak faith to strengthen
   For the last weariness, the final strife.

"We would see Jesus"—for life's hand hath rested
  With its dark touch upon both heart and brow!
And though our souls have many a billow breasted
  Others are rising in the distance now.

"We would see Jesus"—the great rock foundation,
  Whereon our feet were set by sovereign grace;
Not life, nor death, with all their agitation,
  Shall thence remove us, if we see His face.

"We would see Jesus"—other lights are paling,
  Which for long years we have rejoiced to see;
The blessings of our pilgrimage are failing,
  We would not mourn them, for we go to Thee.

"We would see Jesus"—yet the spirit lingers
  Round the dear objects it has loved so long;
And earth from earth can scarce unclose its fingers,
  Our love to Thee makes not this love less strong.

"We would see Jesus"—sense is all too blinding,
  And heaven appears too dim—too far away,
We would see Thee, to gain a sweet reminding,
  That Thou hast promised our great debt to pay.

"We would see Jesus"—this is all we're needing;
  Strength, joy, and willingness come with the sight:
"We would see Jesus"—dying, risen, pleading;
  Then welcome day, and farewell mortal night.

The Sleep of Death.

CALM on the bosom of thy God,
    Fair spirit! rest thee now!
E'en while with us thy footstep trod,
    His seal was on thy brow.

Dust, to its narrow house beneath!
    Soul, to its place on high!
They who have seen thy look in death
    No more may fear to die.

Lone are the paths, and sad the bowers,
    Whence thy meek smile is gone;
But oh! a brighter home than ours,
    In heaven is now thine own.

Hemans.

"She is not dead, but sleepeth."

    The baby wept;
The mother took it from the nurse's arms,
And soothed its grief, and stilled its vain alarms,
    And baby slept.

    Again it weeps;
And God doth take it from the mother's arms,
From present pain, and future unknown harms,
    And baby sleeps.

Hinds.

Heaven.

OH talk to me of heaven, I love
To hear about my home above,
For there doth many a loved one dwell,
In light and joy ineffable.
Oh tell me how they shine and sing,
While every harp rings echoing ;
While every glad and tearless eye
Beams like the bright sun gloriously.
Tell me of that celestial calm
Each face in glory weareth,
Tell me of that victorious palm
Each hand in glory beareth.

Oh happy, happy country, where
There enters not a sin,
And death, who keeps the portals fair,
May never once come in ;
No grief can change their day to night,
The darkness of that land is light,
Sorrow and sighing God has sent
Far thence to endless banishment.
And never more may one dark tear
Bedim their burning eyes,
For every one they shed while here
In fearful agonies,
Glitters a bright and dazzling gem
In their immortal diadem.

O lovely blooming country, there
Flourishes all that we deem fair.
For though no fields nor forests green,
Nor bowery gardens there are seen,
Nor perfumes load the breeze,
Nor hears the ear material sound,
Yet joys at God's right hand are found,
The archetypes of these.

This is the home, the land of birth
Of all we highest prize on earth ;
The storms that rack this world beneath
Shall there for ever cease,
The only air the blessed breathe
Is purity and peace.
Oh may heaven's gate unclose to me,
Oh may I too its glories see,
And my faint, fighting spirit stand
Within that happy, happy land.

At Home in Heaven.

"For ever with the Lord !"
    Amen ; so let it be ;
Life from the dead is in that word,
    'Tis immortality.

Here in the body pent,
    Absent from Him I roam,
Yet nightly pitch my moving tent
    A day's march nearer home.

My Father's house on high,
   Home of my soul, how near,
At times, to faith's far-seeing eye,
   Thy golden gates appear!

Ah! then my spirit faints
   To reach the land I love,
The bright inheritance of saints,
   Jerusalem above.

Yet clouds will intervene,
   And all my prospect flies;
Like Noah's dove, I flit between
   Rough seas and stormy skies.

Anon the clouds dispart,
   The winds and waters cease,
While sweetly o'er my gladdened heart
   Expands the bow of peace.

Beneath its glowing arch,
   Along the hallowed ground,
I see cherubic armies march,
   A camp of fire around.

I hear at morn and even,
   At noon and midnight hour,
The choral harmonies of heaven
   Earth's Babel tongues o'erpower.

Then, then I feel that He,
   (Remembered or forgot,)
The Lord is never far from me,
   Though I perceive Him not.

In darkness as in light,
   Hidden alike from view,
I sleep, I wake, as in His sight
   Who looks all nature through.

From the dim hour of birth,
   Through every changing state
Of mortal pilgrimage on earth,
   Till its appointed date.

All that I am, have been,
   All that I yet may be,
He sees at once, as He hath seen,
   And shall for ever see.

How can I meet His eyes?
   Mine on the cross I cast,
And own my life a Saviour's prize,
   Mercy from first to last.

"For ever with the Lord!"
   Father, if 'tis Thy will,
The promise of that faithful word,
   E'en here to me fulfil.

Be Thou at my right hand,
   Then can I never fail;
Uphold Thou me, and I shall stand;
   Fight, and I must prevail.

So when my latest breath
   Shall rend the veil in twain,
By death I shall escape from death,
   And life eternal gain.

Knowing as I am known,
   How shall I love that word,
And oft repeat before the throne,
   "For ever with the Lord."

Then though the soul enjoy
   Communion high and sweet,
While worms this body must destroy,
   Both shall in glory meet.

The trump of final doom
   Will speak the self-same word,
And heaven's voice thunder through the
   tomb,
   "For ever with the Lord."

The tomb shall echo deep
   That death-awakening sound;
The saints shall hear it in their sleep,
   And answer from the ground.

Then, upward as they fly,
   That resurrection-word
Shall be their shout of victory,
   " For ever with the Lord."

That resurrection-word,
   That shout of victory,
Once more, " For ever with the Lord !"
   Amen, so let it be !

Montgomery.

His Servants shall serve Him.

WE seek that land whose light e'en now,
   Though dimmed and far, is all our gladness,
Whose hope, in storms, is God's own bow,
Whose peace, the rest from care and woe,
   Whose love, our joy in sadness.

There day and night Thy happy saints
   In ceaseless work, find rest unending,
Where in Thy strength theirs never faints,
Where tears are dried, and hushed complaints,
   All in one worship bending.

The service here we strive to pay
   By weakness marred, by darkness clouded,
Strong in Thy strength, bright with Thy day,
We there shall offer perfectly,
   In light and love unshrouded.

Our hearts, whose love has taught them this,
   Their wants to feel, their own unmeetness,
Shall learn in that ne'er ending bliss,
To rise towards Thine own perfectness,
   Thine infinite completeness.

The songs, here drowned in the moan
   Of earth's unrest, which ceaseth never,
Shall rise in strains of joy unknown,
To Him who sitteth on the throne,
   And to the Lamb for ever.

And for our feet, to earth which cling,
   Feeble and slow, too oft unwilling,
Thou there shalt give an angel's wing
To serve, as angels do, our King,
   Thy high behests fulfilling.

So let us strive, with earnest soul,
   Thy work to do, though small the measure,
Knowing it part of one great whole,
All tending to our highest goal,
   Thy perfect will and pleasure.

L. R.

And they shall see His face.

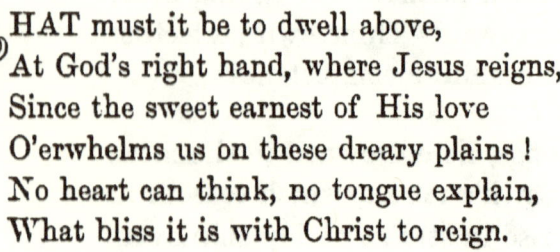HAT must it be to dwell above,
At God's right hand, where Jesus reigns,
Since the sweet earnest of His love
O'erwhelms us on these dreary plains!
No heart can think, no tongue explain,
What bliss it is with Christ to reign.

When sin no more obstructs our sight,
When sorrow pains our heart no more,
How shall we view the Prince of Light,
And all His works of grace explore!
What heights and depths of love divine
Will there through endless ages shine!

Well, He has fixed the happy day
When the last tears will wet our eyes,
And God shall wipe those tears away,
And fill us with divine surprise
To hear His voice, and see His face,
And feel His infinite embrace!

This is the heaven I long to know;
For this, with patience, I would wait,
Till, weaned from earth and all below,
I mount to my celestial seat,
And wave my palm, and wear my crown,
And, with the elders, cast them down.

Swain.

Who shall ascend to the holy place?

WHO shall ascend to the holy place,
  And stand on the holy hill?
Who shall the boundless realms of space
  With shouts of rapture thrill?
          Hallelujah! Hallelujah!
For the Lord God omnipotent reigneth!

The servants of the Lord are they,
  The pure in heart and hand,
For whom the eternal bars give way,
  The eternal gates expand!
          Hallelujah! &c.

Not to the noble, not to the strong,
  To the wealthy, or the wise,
Is given a part in that angel-song,
  That music of the skies;
          Hallelujah! &c.

But those who, in humble and holy fear,
  With child-like faith and love,
Have served the Lord as their Master here,
  Shall praise their Lord above.
          Hallelujah! &c.

And chiefly those who in youth to Him
   Their morn of life have given,
With Cherubim and Seraphim,
   And all the host of heaven,
               Hallelujah ! &c.

Shall stand in robes of purest white;
   And to the Lamb shall raise
The song that rests not day or night,
   The eternity of praise.
               Hallelujah ! &c.
                  Hankinson.

The City of our God.

GLORIOUS things of thee are spoken,
   Zion, city of our God !
He, whose word cannot be broken,
   Formed thee for His own abode :
On the Rock of Ages founded,
   What can shake thy sure repose ?
With salvation's wall surrounded,
   Thou may'st smile at all thy foes.

See ! the streams of living waters
   Springing from eternal love,
Well supply thy sons and daughters,
   And all fear of want remove :

Who can faint while such a river
   Ever flows, their thirst to assuage ?
Grace, which like the Lord, the Giver,
   Never fails from age to age.

Round each habitation hovering,
   See the cloud and fire appear !
For a glory and a covering,
   Showing that the Lord is near ;
Thus deriving from their banner,
   Light by night and shade by day,
Safe they feed upon the manna
   Which He gives them when they pray.

Blest inhabitants of Zion,
   Washed in the Redeemer's blood !
Jesus, whom their souls rely on,
   Makes them kings and priests to God :
'Tis His love His people raises,
   Over self to reign as kings ;
And, as priests, his solemn praises
   Each for a thank-offering brings.

Saviour, if of Zion's city
   I through grace a member am ;
Let the world deride or pity,
   I will glory in Thy name :

Fading is the worldling's pleasure,
  All his boasted pomp and show;
Solid joys and lasting treasure,
  None but Zion's children know.

Newton.

Bought with a price.

SAVIOUR of men, and Lord of love,
  How sweet Thy gracious name!
With joy that errand we review
  On which Thy mercy came.

While all Thine own angelic bands
  Stood waiting on the wing,
Charmed with the honour to obey
  The word of such a King,—

For us, mean, wretched, sinful men,
  Thou laidst that glory by,
First in our mortal flesh to serve,
  Then in that flesh to die.

Bought with Thy service and Thy blood,
  We doubly, Lord, are Thine;
To Thee our lives we would devote,
  To Thee our death resign.

Doddridge.

He had not where to lay His head.

BIRDS have their quiet nest,
    Foxes their holes, and man his peaceful bed;
All creatures have their rest,
    But Jesus had not where to lay His head.

    Winds have their hour of calm,
And waves, to slumber on the voiceless deep:
    Eve hath its breath of balm,
To hush all senses and all sounds to sleep.

    The wild deer hath its lair,
The homeward flocks the shelter of their shed;
    All have their rest from care,—
But Jesus had not where to lay His head.

    And yet He came to give
The weary and the heavy-laden rest;
    To bid the sinner live,
And soothe my griefs to slumber on His breast.

    What then am I, my God,
Permitted thus the paths of peace to tread?
    Peace, purchased by the blood
Of Him who had not where to lay His head.

    I, who once made Him grieve,
I, who once made His gentle spirit mourn;
    Whose hand essayed to weave
For His meek brow the cruel crown of thorn:—

  O why should I have peace?
Why? but for that unchanged, undying love,
  Which would not, could not cease,
Until it made me heir of joys above.

  Yes, but for pardoning grace,
I feel I never should in glory see
  The brightness of that face,
That once was pale and agonized for me.

  Let the birds seek their nest,
Foxes their holes, and man his peaceful bed;
  Come, Saviour, in my breast
Deign to repose Thine oft rejected head!

  On earth Thou lovest best
To dwell in humble souls that mourn for sin!
  O come and take Thy rest,
This broken, bleeding, contrite heart within.
J. S. Monsell.

The Righteous Advocate.

FATHER, I bring this worthless child to Thee,
To claim Thy pardon, once, yet once again.
Receive him at my hand, for he is mine.
He is a worthless child; he owns his fault;
Look not on him, he will not bear the glance;
Look but on me, I'll hide his filthy garments.
He pleads not for himself, he dares not plead;
His cause is mine, I am his Intercessor.

By that unchanged, unchanging love of Thine,
By each pure drop of blood I shed for him,
By all the sorrows graven on my soul,
By every wound I bear, I claim it true.
Father divine! I would not have him lost;
He is a worthless child, but he is mine!
Sin hath destroyed him—sin hath died in me;
Satan hath bound him—Satan is my slave;
Death hath desired him—I have conquered death.
My Father, hear him now, not him, but me!
I would not have him lost for all the worlds
Which Thou hast long created for my glory,
Because he is a poor, a worthless child,
And all his every hope on me it lies,
I know my children, and I know him mine.
By all the sighs he pours o'er outcast Israel,
By all the prayers he breathes o'er Judah's sins,
I know him by the sign my children bear,
That trusting love by which he cleaves to me.
I could not bear to see him cast away,
Vile as he is! the weakest of my flock,
The one that grieves me most and loves me least.
Yes! tho' his sins dim every spark of love,
I measure not my love by his returns,
And though the stripes I send to bring him home
Should seem to drive him further from my arms,
Still he is mine! I lured him from the world;
He has no right, no home, but in my love.
Tho' earth and hell combined against him rise

I'm bound to rescue him, for we are one.
  Oh, sinner! what an Advocate is thine;
Methinks I see Him lead the captive in,
Poor, sorrowful, ashamed, trembling with fear,
Shrinking behind his Lord, accused, condemned,
Well pleased to hide the form himself abhors
With that all-spotless garment of his Friend.
But look! some secret impulse lifts his eye,
To see if love be mingled now with wrath,
If mercy beams upon the Father's face.
Poor sinner! read thy welcome in that smile,
And hear the Father's word to him for thee,
"Take Thy poor worthless child! I have forgiven."

E. Birrell.

"As many as touched were made perfectly whole."

SAVIOUR divine, we bend before Thee lowly,
Sadly we bring into Thy presence holy
  Our hearts, so sin-oppressed;
Touching the border of Thy garment pure,
Whose touch all sorrow and all sin can cure,
  We ask Thee for Thy rest.

And in so stooping, higher shall we reach
Than e'en the highest point our hearts can teach,
  Even dear Lord to Thee,
Whose lowliness hath raised us to such height,
That we may dare to touch Thy garment white,
  Of matchless purity.

Thy gentleness, O Christ, hath made us great
Thy uncrown'd majesty our lost estate
   Redeemed by bitter woe;
And though our trembling fingers feebly hold,
Yea, scarcely touch Thy holy garment's fold,
   Thou wilt not let us go.

Thy love, the source of ours, shall still abide,
Shall draw us, wandering, closer to Thy side,
   And make us wholly pure;
Led ever higher by its light divine,
Wrapped in its heavenly beauty shall we shine,
   In love and rest secure.

L. R.

"Create in me a clean heart."

OH for a heart to praise my God,
   A heart from sin set free;
A heart that's sprinkled with the blood
   So freely shed for me!

A heart resigned, submissive, meek,
   My dear Redeemer's throne:
Where only Christ is heard to speak,
   Where Jesus reigns alone!

A lowly and believing heart,
   Abhorring every sin;
Which neither life nor death can part,
   From Him that dwells within.

A heart in every thought renewed,
   And filled with love divine;
Perfect, and right, and pure, and good;
   A copy, Lord, of Thine.

Thy nature, gracious Lord, impart,
   Come quickly from above:
Write Thy new name upon my heart,
   Thy new, best name of LOVE.

"Renew a right spirit within me."

GRACIOUS Spirit, dwell with me,
I myself would gracious be;
And with words that help and heal,
Would Thy life in mine reveal:
And with actions bold and meek,
Would for Christ, my Saviour, speak.

Truthful Spirit, dwell with me,
I myself would truthful be;
And with wisdom kind and clear,
Let Thy life in mine appear,
And with actions brotherly,
Speak my Lord's sincerity.

Tender Spirit, dwell with me,
I myself would tender be;

Shut my heart up like a flower
At temptation's darksome hour;
Open it when shines the sun,
And his love by fragrance own.

Silent Spirit, dwell with me,
I myself would quiet be,
Quiet as the growing blade
That through earth its way has made,
Silently, like morning light,
Putting mists and chills to flight.

Mighty Spirit, dwell with me,
I myself would mighty be;
Mighty so as to prevail
Where, unaided, man must fail;
Ever by a mighty hope,
Pressing on and bearing up.

Holy Spirit, dwell with me,
I myself would holy be;
Separate from sin, I would
Choose and cherish all things good,
And whatever I can be,
Give to Him, who gave me Thee.

Lynch.

"Lovest thou Me."

"LOVEST thou Me?" I hear my Saviour say:
Would that my heart had power to answer "yea,
"Thou knowest all things, Lord, in heaven above
"And earth beneath; Thou knowest that I love."

But 'tis not so; in word, in deed, in thought,
I do not, cannot, love Thee as I ought;
Thy love must give that power, Thy love alone;
There's nothing worthy of Thee but Thine own;
Lord, with the love wherewith Thou lovest me,
Reflected on Thyself, I would love Thee.

J. Montgomery.

Hide me under the shadow of Thy wings.

STILL nigh me, O my Saviour, stand,
And guard in fierce temptation's hour;
Hide in the hollow of Thy hand;
Show forth in me Thy saving power:
Still be Thine arm my sure defence,
Nor earth nor hell shall pluck me thence.

In suffering be Thy love my peace!
In weakness be Thy love my power!
And when the storms of life shall cease,
Jesus, in that important hour,
In death, as life, be Thou my guide,
And save me, who for me hast died.

The House of God.

"Surely the Lord is in this place, and I knew it not." Gen. xxviii, 16.

SINCE slow and sad the evening fell
On desert path, on lonely dell,
  As, sad and desolate,
One laid him down to sleep alone,
His couch the sand, his pillow stone,
  The morning-tide to wait.

But gleamed before his dazzled sight
A radiance more than morning light,
  From opened portals given;
And on his charmèd ear there rung
A sound more sweet than matin song—
  The choral hymns of heaven.

He saw the glory of that place
Whose light is God the Saviour's face,
  He saw its dwellers fair;
And learnt that—desolate, alone,
A wanderer from his Father's home,—
  God's presence still was there.

So we, (though often worn, oppressed,
We wander, seeking home and rest,)
  In sorrow's darkest hour
May see, as Jacob saw of old,
God's sunbeams bright and manifold,
  The shades of night o'erpower.

For not in temple hoar alone,
In cloistered shade, 'neath sculptured stone,
   Stands now God's house below;
But wheresoe'er His radiance bright
Gleams on our darkness and 'tis light,
   His presence we may know.

Transfigured in His glory fair
The whole earth stands, one house of prayer,
   One ante-room of heaven;
For surely, though we know it not,
God's presence is in every spot,
   To those who seek it given.

Then let us strive, and work, and wait,
As those who see that opened gate,
   That glory in our night;
So that at last, through Christ the way,
We too may tread that land of day,
   Where God, the Lord, is light.

L. R.

Paraphrase on Psalm lxxxiv.

PLEASANT are Thy courts above,
In the land of light and love;
Pleasant are Thy courts below,
In this land of sin and woe,
Oh, my spirit longs and faints
For the converse of Thy saints;

For the brightness of Thy face,
King of glory, God of grace.

Happy birds that sing and fly
Round Thine altars, O most High!
Happier souls that find a rest
In a heavenly Father's breast!
Like the wandering dove that found
No repose on earth around,
They can to their ark repair,
And enjoy it ever there.

Happy souls, their praises flow
Ever in this vale of woe;
Waters in the desert rise,
Manna feeds them from the skies;
On they go from strength to strength,
Till they reach Thy throne at length,
At Thy feet adoring fall,
Who hast led them safe through all.

Lord, be mine this prize to win,
Guide me through a world of sin,
Keep me by Thy saving grace,
Give me at Thy side a place.
Sun and shield alike Thou art;
Guide and guard my erring heart;
Grace and glory flow from Thee;
Shower, oh shower them, Lord, on me.

H. F. Lyte.

The Exile's Vision.

THE blue Egean's countless waves in Sabbath
    sunlight smiled,
And murmuring washed the rocky shore of
    that lone island wild;
Where unto him "whom Jesus loved," such
    views sublime were given,
That e'en the land of exile shone "the very
    gate of heaven!"

He saw the radiant form of Him, upon
    whose sorrowing breast,
At the last supper's solemn feast his weary
    head found rest;
One "like unto the Son of man," all glorious
    to behold,
Arrayed in robes of dazzling light, and girt
    with purest gold.

His head and hair were white as wool; His
    eyes a fiery flame,
Not tearful now as when He trod this world
    of sin and shame;
His countenance was as the sun, His voice
    was as the sound
Of many waters, murmuring deep in harmony
    profound.

Christian Lyrics.

But when before His feet as dead, the loved
    disciple fell,
How gently deigned the Prince of life His
    servant's fears to quell!
And gave him strength to see His face, whom
    highest heavens adore,
The Lord, who "liveth, and was dead," and
    lives for evermore!

Oh! then upon his raptured gaze what
    floods of glory streamed;
He saw the land of love and light—the
    home of the redeemed;
He stood by life's resplendent stream, whose
    tide in music rolled
Throughout the holy city's length among its
    streets of gold.

He heard the mighty new-made song, to
    angel-hosts unknown,
Go up like incense unto Him that sat upon
    the throne;
And the pure strains by seraphs sung in that
    celestial sphere,
In sweetest cadence rose and fell upon his
    listening ear.

Within the flashing walls of heaven, with
    jewelled splendour bright,
He saw the countless multitudes arrayed
    in saintly white;

He marked them with their waving palms,
    in worship bending low
Before the feet of Him who smil'd beneath
    the emerald bow.

The pearly gates, the crystal sea, the
    universal hymn,
The sun-bright forms, the brilliant eyes,
    which tears may never dim,
The healing trees, the fadeless flowers, the
    harpings of the blest,
In splendid vision to his soul revealed the
    promised rest.

Long since that aged saint hath reached the
    fair celestial shore,
And gained the martyr's crown, for he the
    martyr's suffering bore;
Long since his happy feet have stood within
    his Father's home,
Yet *still* the mighty voice he heard, with
    ceaseless cry, saith, "Come!"

And life's bright fountain springeth yet, as
    free, and fresh, and fair,
As when in Patmos' dreary isle it cheered
    the exile there!
And hark! the Spirit and the Bride repeat
    in mercy still,
That he who is athirst may drink—yea,
    whosoever will!

O blessed voices! be it ours your loving call
    to hear
And so obey that when, at last, from yonder
    radiant sphere
The heavenly bridegroom shall descend to
    claim His own again,
We may lift up our heads and say, "Lord
    even so, Amen!"

Sunday at Home.

Sabbath Morning.

LIGHT of lights enlighten me
    Now anew the day is dawning;
Sun of grace, the shadows flee,
    Brighten Thou my sabbath morning,
With Thy joyous sunshine blest,
Happy is my day of rest.

Fount of all our joy and peace,
    To Thy living waters lead me,
Thou from earth my soul release,
    And with grace and mercy feed me;
Bless Thy word that it may prove
Rich in fruits that Thou dost love.

Kindle Thou the sacrifice
    That upon my lips is lying;
Clear the shadows from mine eyes,
    That, from every error flying,
No strange fire may in me glow
That Thine altar doth not know.

Let me, with my heart to-day
    Holy, holy, holy, singing,
Rapt awhile from earth away,
    All my soul to Thee upspringing,
Have a foretaste inly given
How they worship Thee in heaven.

Rest in me and I in Thee,
    Build a paradise within me;
O reveal Thyself to me,
    Blessed love, who diedst to win me;
Fed by Thine exhaustless urn,
Pure and bright my lamp shall burn.

Hence all care, all vanity,
    For the day to God is holy;
Come, thou glorious majesty,
    Deign to fill this temple lowly,
Nought to-day my soul shall move,
Simply resting in Thy love.

                              Lyra Germanica.

Communion with God.

LORD, I am come alone with Thee!
Thy voice to hear, Thy face to see,
   And feel Thy presence near;
It is not fancy's lovely dream,
Though wondrous e'en to faith it seem,
   That Thou dost wait me here.

A moment from this outward life,
Its service, self-denial, strife,
   I joyfully retreat,
My soul, through intercourse with Thee,
Strengthened, refreshed, and calmed shall be,
   Its scenes again to meet.

How can it be that one so mean,
A sinner, selfish, dark, unclean,
   Thus in the holiest stands;
And in that light divinely pure,
Which may no stain of sin endure,
   Lifts up rejoicing hands.

Jesus! the answer Thou hast given!
Thy death, Thy life, have opened heaven,
   And all its joys to me;
Washed in Thy blood—oh wondrous grace!
I'm holy as the holy place
   In which I worship Thee.

How sweet, how solemn, thus to lie
And feel Jehovah's searching eye
  On me well pleased can rest!
Because with His beloved Son
The Father's grace has made me one,
  I must be always blest.

The secret pangs I could not tell
To dearest friend,—*Thou* knowest well,
  They claim Thy gracious heart;
Thou dost remove with tender care,
Or sweetly give me strength to bear,
  The sanctifying smart.

Thy presence has a wondrous power;
The sharpest thorn becomes a flower,
  And breathes a sweet perfume;
Whate'er looked dark and sad before,
With happy light shines silvered o'er,—
  There's no such thing as gloom!

Thou knowest I have a cross to bear:
The needful stroke Thou dost not spare,
  To keep me near Thy side;
But when I see Thy chastening rod
In Thy pierced hand, my Lord, my God,
  I feel so satisfied!

Charlotte Wilkins.

In Suffering.

FATHER, Thy will, not mine, be done;
So prayed on earth Thy suffering Son;
   So in His name I pray.
The spirit faints, the flesh is weak,
Thy help in agony I seek,
   Oh! take this cup away.

  If such be not Thy sovereign will,
  Thy wiser purpose then fulfil;
     My wishes I resign;
  Into Thy hands my soul commend,
  On Thee for life or death depend;
     Thy will be done, not mine.

Clear Shining after Rain.

COMETH sunshine after rain,
After mourning joy again,
After heavy bitter grief
Dawneth surely sweet relief!
   And my soul, who from her height
   Sank to realms of woe and night,
   Wingeth now to heaven her flight.

None was ever left a prey,
None was ever turned away,
Who had given himself to God,
And on Him had cast his load.
    Who in God his hope hath placed
    Shall not life in pain out-waste,
    Fullest joy he yet shall taste.

Though to-day may not fulfil
All thy hopes, have patience still,
For perchance to-morrow's sun
Sees thy happier days begun;
    As God willeth march the hours,
    Bringing joy at last in showers,
    When whate'er we asked is ours.

Every sorrow, every smart,
That the eternal Father's heart
Hath appointed me of yore,
Or hath yet for me in store,
    As my life flows on I'll take
    Calmly, gladly for His sake,
    No more faithless murmurs make.

I will meet distress and pain,
I will greet e'en death's dark reign,
I will lay me in the grave,
With a heart still glad and brave;
    Whom the Strongest doth defend,
    Whom the Highest counts His friend,
    Cannot perish in the end.

Lyra Germanica.

Songs of Praise.

Songs of praise the angels sang,
Heaven with hallelujahs rang,
When Jehovah's work begun,
When He spake and it was done.

Songs of praise awoke the morn,
When the Prince of peace was born;
Songs of praise arose, when He
Captive led captivity.

Heaven and earth must pass away,
Songs of praise shall crown that day:
God will make new heavens and earth,
Songs of praise shall hail their birth.

And will man alone be dumb,
Till that glorious kingdom come?
No :—the church delights to raise
Psalms, and hymns, and songs of praise.

Saints below, with heart and voice,
Still in songs of praise rejoice;
Learning here by faith and love,
Songs of praise to sing above.

Borne upon their latest breath,
Songs of praise shall conquer death;
Then amidst eternal joy
Songs of praise their powers employ.

Montgomery.

The Angel of Patience.

TRANSLATED FROM THE GERMAN.

THROUGHOUT this earth in stillness
    An angel walks abroad,
For consoling in our weakness
    He is strengthened of the Lord;
Peace in his look abideth,
    With a mild and quiet grace,
Oh! follow where he guideth,
    Follow Patience in thy race.

He ever truly leads thee
    Through suffering here below,
And, speaking oft to cheer thee,
    A brighter time he'll show.
Does thy heart sink despairing?
    Thy hope he doth recall,
He helps thee in cross-bearing,
    To good he turneth all.

He calms to quiet sadness
    The anguish of thy breast;
The heart that was so restless,
    In humility hath rest.
Thy darkest hour of weeping
    He brighteneth by degrees,
Though thy wound be slow in healing,
    He gives thee certain ease.

Thy tears no anger cause him,
  He waiteth to console,
He chides not thy desiring,
  With grace he stills thy soul.
When troubles round are raging,
  Murm'ring, thou askest "why?"
Voiceless—thy grief assuaging,
  He smiles and points on high.

Not for all anxious questions
  Doth he replies prepare,
The sum of his monitions,
  "Endure—soon ends thy care."
Thus, with thy footsteps blending,
  His words are few and plain,
And his thoughts are only tending
  To the great, the glorious aim.

M. S. M.

Incompleteness.

NOTHING resting in its own completeness
Can have worth or beauty: but alone
Because it leads and tends to farther sweetness,
Fuller, higher, deeper than its own.

Spring's real glory dwells not in the meaning,
Gracious though it be, of her blue hours;
But is hidden in her tender leaning
To the summer's richer wealth of flowers.

Dawn is fair because the mists fade slowly
Into day, which floods the world with light;
Twilight's mystery is so sweet and holy,
Just because it ends in starry night.

Childhood's smiles unconscious graces borrow
From strife, that in a far-off future lies;
And angel glances (veiled now by life's sorrow)
Draw our hearts to some beloved eyes.

Life is only bright when it proceedeth
Towards a truer, deeper life above;
Human love is sweetest when it leadeth
To a more divine and perfect love.

Learn the mystery of progression duly,
Do not call each glorious change decay;
But know we only hold our treasures truly
When it seems as if they passed away;

Nor dare to blame God's gifts for incompleteness;
In that want their beauty lies: they roll
Towards some infinite depth of love and sweetness,
Bearing onwards man's reluctant soul.

A. A. Procter.

Nearer to Thee.

NEARER, my God, to Thee,—
    Nearer to Thee,
E'en though it be a cross
    That raiseth me:
Still all my song would be,
Nearer, my God, to Thee,
    Nearer to Thee.

Though like the wanderer,
    Daylight all gone,
Darkness be o'er me,
    My rest a stone;
Yet, in my dreams, I'd be
Nearer, my God, to Thee,
    Nearer to Thee.

There let the way appear
    Steps unto heaven;
All that Thou sendest me,
    In mercy given;
Angels to beckon me
Nearer, my God, to Thee,
    Nearer to Thee.

Then with my waking thoughts
    Bright with Thy praise,
Out of my stony griefs
    Bethel I'll raise;
So by my woes to be
Nearer, my God, to Thee,
    Nearer to Thee.

Or if on joyful wing,
    Cleaving the sky,
Sun, moon, and stars forgot,
    Upwards I fly;
Still all my song shall be,
Nearer, my God, to Thee,
    Nearer to Thee.

Christ alone beareth me
    Where Thou dost shine:
Joint-heir He maketh me
    Of the Divine!
In Christ my soul shall be
Nearer, my God, to Thee,
    Nearer to Thee.

S. F. Adams.

Tribulation worketh Patience.

As the harp strings only render
    All their treasures of sweet sound,
All their music, glad or tender,
    Firmly struck or tightly bound.

So the hearts of Christians owe
    Each its deepest, sweetest strain,
To the pressure firm of woe,
    And the tension tight of pain.

Spices crushed their pungence yield,
    Trodden scents their sweets respire;
Would you have its strength revealed,
    Cast the incense in the fire.

Thus the crushed and broken frame
    Oft doth sweetest graces yield;
And through suffering, toil, and shame,
From the martyr's keenest flame,
    Heavenly incense is distill'd!

The Voice of Christian Life in Song.

Clinging to Thee.

HOLY Saviour, Friend unseen,
Since on Thine arm Thou bidst me lean,
Help me, throughout life's varying scene,
  By faith to cling to Thee!

Blest with this fellowship divine,
Take what Thou wilt, I'll ne'er repine,
E'en as the branches to the vine
  My soul would cling to Thee!

Far from her home, fatigued, opprest,
Here she has found her place of rest;
An exile still, yet not unblest,
  While she can cling to Thee!

Without a murmur I dismiss
My former dreams of earthly bliss;
My joy, my consolation this,
  Each hour to cling to Thee!

What though the world deceitful prove,
And earthly friends and joys remove;
With patient, uncomplaining love
  Still would I cling to Thee!

Oft when I seem to tread alone
Some barren waste with thorns o'ergrown,
Thy voice of love, in tenderest tone,
  Whispers "Still cling to Me;"

Though faith and hope awhile be tried
I ask not, need not, aught beside:
How safe, how calm, how satisfied,
      The souls that cling to Thee!

They fear not Satan or the grave,
They feel Thee near and strong to save,
Nor fear to cross e'en Jordan's wave,
      Because they cling to Thee!

Blest is my lot, whate'er befall;
What can disturb me, what appal,
Whilst as my Rock, my Strength, my All,
      Saviour, I cling to Thee?

Cast down but not destroyed.

MUCH have I borne, but not as I should bear;
The proud will unsubdued, the formal prayer,
Tell me Thou yet wilt chide, Thou canst not spare,
      O Lord, Thy chastening rod!
O help me, Father, for my sinful heart
Back from this discipline of grief would start,
Unmindful of His sorer, deeper smart,
      Who died for me, my God!

Yet if each wish denied, each woe and pain,
Break but some link of that oppressive chain
Which binds us still to earth, and leaves a stain
        Thou only canst remove—
Then am I blest—O bliss from man concealed!
If here to Christ, the weak one's tower and shield,
My heart through sorrow be set free to yield
        A service of deep love.
F. F.

Thankfulness.

MY God, I thank Thee who hast made
    The earth so bright;
So full of splendour and of joy,
    Beauty and light;
So many glorious things are here,
    Noble and right.

I thank Thee, too, that Thou hast made
    Joy to abound;
So many gentle thoughts and deeds
    Circling us around,
That in the darkest spot of earth
    Some love is found.

I thank Thee more, that all our joy
    Is touched with pain;
That shadows fall on brightest hours,
    That thorns remain;

So that earth's bliss may be our guide,
    And not our chain.

For Thou who knowest, Lord, how soon
    Our weak heart clings,
Hast given us joys, tender and true,
    Yet all with wings,
So that we see gleaming on high
    Diviner things.

I thank thee, Lord, that Thou hast kept
    The best in store;
We have enough, yet not too much
    To long for more:
A yearning for a deeper peace
    Not known before.

I thank Thee, Lord, that here our souls,
    Though amply blest,
Can never find, although they seek,
    A perfect rest—
Nor ever shall, until they lean
    On Jesus' breast.

A. A. Procter.

Contentment.

SOME murmur, when their sky is clear
    And wholly bright to view,
If one small speck of dark appear
    In their great heaven of blue:
And some with thankful love are filled
    If but one streak of light,
One ray of God's good mercy gild
    The darkness of their night.

In palaces are hearts that ask,
    In discontent and pride,
Why life is such a dreary task
    And all good things denied?
And hearts in poorest huts admire
    How love has in their aid
(Love that not ever seems to tire)
    Such rich provision made.

R. C. Trench.

Midnight Hymn.

IN the mid silence of the voiceless night,
When, chased by airy dreams, the slumbers flee,
Whom in the darkness doth my spirit seek,
    O God, but Thee?

And if there be a weight upon my breast,
Some vague impression of the day foregone,
Scarce knowing what it is, I fly to Thee,
     And lay it down.

Or if it be the heaviness that comes
In token of anticipated ill—
My bosom takes no heed of what it is,
     Since 'tis Thy will.

For oh! in spite of past and present care,
Or anything beside—how joyfully
Passes that silent solitary hour,
     My God with Thee!

More tranquil than the stillness of the night,
More peaceful than the silence of that hour,
More blest than anything, my bosom lies
     Beneath Thy power.

For what is there on earth that I desire,
Of all that it can give or take from me?
Or whom in heaven doth my spirit seek,
     O God, but Thee?

Morning Hymn.

COME, my soul, awake, 'tis morning,
    Day is dawning
O'er the earth, arise and pray,
Come to Him who made this splendour,
    Thou must render
All thy feeble powers can pay.

From the stars now learn thy duty,
    See their beauty
Paling in the golden air;
So God's light thy mists should banish,
    Thus should vanish
What to darkened sense seemed fair.

See how every thing that liveth,
    Gladly striveth
On the pleasant light to gaze;
Stirs with joy each thing that groweth,
    As it knoweth,
Darkness smitten by these rays.

Soul, thy incense also proffer,
    Thou shouldst offer
Praise to Him, who from thy head
Kept afar the storms of sorrow,
    And the morrow
Finds the night in peace hath fled.

Bid Him bless what thou art doing,
 If pursuing
Some good end; but if there lurks
Ill intent in thine endeavour,
 May He ever
Thwart and turn thee from thy works.

Think that He, the All-discerning,
 Knows each turning
Of thy path, each sinful stain;
Nay, what shame would fain gloss over,
 Can discover;
All thou dost to Him is plain.

Bound unto the flying hours
 Are our powers;
Earth's vain good floats down their wave,
That thy ship, my soul, is hasting,
 Never resting,
To its haven in the grave.

Pray that when thy life is closing,
 Calm reposing,
Thou may'st die, and not in pain;
That, the night of death departed,
 Thou glad-hearted
May'st behold the sun again.

From God's glances shrink thou never,
 Meet them ever;
Who submits him to His grace,

Finds that earth no sunshine knoweth
    Such as gloweth
O'er his pathway all his days.

Wakenest thou again to sorrow,
    Oh! then borrow
Strength from Him, whose sunlike might
On the mountain summit tarries,
    And yet carries
To the vales their mirth and light.

Round the gifts He on thee showers,
    Fiery towers
Will He set; be not afraid,
Thou shalt dwell 'mid angel legions,
    In the regions
Satan's self dares not invade.

Lyra Germanica.

"Pray without ceasing."

"And he spake a parable unto this end, that men ought always to pray and not to faint."

'TWAS long ago in olden time,
Christ spake a parable divine,
    To teach the waiting throng
That men ought evermore to pray,
And God would hear and help alway,
    Although they waited long.

That human voice we may not hear,
That music breaks not on our ear,
   Yet still the words are sure;
And many hearts with grief oppressed,
Have found them light, and hope, and rest,
   And trusted there secure.

And rises, Lord, this cry to Thee,
From weary hearts unceasingly,
   "How long, O Lord, how long!
" O Thou the True, the Good, the Great,
" Have mercy on us desolate,
   " Is not Thy sceptre strong?"

So pray they bowed with sorrow down;
While we whom love and gladness crown
   Bend lower still in prayer,
With hearts so full we need to pray
" Oh make us worthy, Lord, alway
   " This weight of love to bear.

" O help us, mid these beams divine,
" To think of Thee from whom they shine,
   " By whom all love is given;
" To know them but reflections bright
" Of glory true and infinite,
   " Which floods the fields of heaven."

And thus in happiness or care,
Still, Lord, to Thee ascends our prayer,

For strength we cry from far;
And learn, as Jesus taught of old,
In toils and troubles manifold,
To trust Thy guiding star.

So lead us, Thou to whom we pray,
That ever nearer day by day
Unto the Christ we come;
And where we see the star abide,
There—surely trusting in our guide,
May find our rest and home.

L. R.

Thy face, Lord, will I seek.

I HEARD the voice of Jesus say,
"Come unto me and rest;
"Lay down, poor weary one, lay down
"Thy head upon my breast;"
I came to Jesus as I was,
Weary, and worn, and sad;
I found in Him a resting place,
And He has made me glad.

I heard the voice of Jesus say,
"Behold I freely give
"The living water, thirsty one,
"Stoop down, and drink, and live;"

I came to Jesus, and I drank
    Of that life-giving stream;
My thirst was quenched, my soul revived,
    And now I live in Him.

I heard the voice of Jesus say,
    "I am this dark world's Light;
"Look unto Me, thy morn shall rise,
    "And all thy day be bright;"
I looked to Jesus and I found
    In Him my radiant Sun;
So in the Light of light I live,
    And glory is begun!

Bonar.

Joseph a type of Christ.

SOLD by them that should have loved thee,
    Prisoner in the heathen's land,
Given by him that best had proved thee
    To the dungeon and the band:—
From the land of flowers, and rain,
Borne to Egypt's dewless plain,
Leaving tent, and pastoral dell,
And the sire that loved thee well,
And the airs on upland breezy,
    Where the scented cedars grow,
For the servant's toil uneasy
    And the captive's weary woe;—

Out of grief to honour risen,
    Winning rapture for thy pain,
And a palace for thy prison,
    And a sceptre for thy chain;—
    Ruling with a gentle art
    Over many a grateful heart,
    Melting with a brother's love
    Those thine anguish could not move—
Wearing graciously thy glory
    Through the land thy wisdom won—
How should Christians read thy story,
    Aged Israel's favoured son?

As the little sapling tender
    Shows the great oak waving proud;
As the cold lake burns with splendour
    From the crimson sunset-cloud;
    So in sufferings of thine
    Trace we out a grief divine,
    And thy sorrows throb and glow
    With a pulse of heavenly woe!
Type thou art of One more holy
    Who His glory laid aside,
Took the form of servant lowly,
    Stooped to suffering man and died.

He was scorned, and sold, and hated
    By the men He came to save,
With a cruel wrath unsated
    Followed to His three days' grave,—

Not one pitying thought for Him,
When His failing eye waxed dim,
Not one note in sympathy
With that love so full and free,
When His tender spirit yearning,
  Wept those tears of God-like grief
O'er the lawless city, spurning
  Help, and safety, and relief.

Now He reigneth high exalted
  Where the white-robed elders stand,
By the great throne rainbow-vaulted
  Each with golden harp in hand,
  Thousand thousand hearts adoring,
  Thousand thousand vials pouring
  Odours sweet of saintly prayers,
  That embalm those heavenly airs,
Round the Lamb once slain and wounded
  Breathing, till that awful hour,
When by heaven's high host surrounded
  He shall come again in power.

For behind each image saintly
  Burns the light of Jesus' name—
As the lines lie dim and faintly
  In the Gothic window frame,
  Till the sunlight touch the pane
  Rising o'er the fretted fane,

And each form and gorgeous hue
   Starts to sight distinct and true.
So doth many a sin-stained creature
   Catch a glory from Christ's face,
And a light is on his feature,
   That our eyes should love to trace.

C. F. A.

Glory to God in the highest.

GLORIOUS was that primeval light
   Which poured its golden flood
O'er the young earth, when fresh and bright
   In its first bloom it stood.

But, lo! another light, that shines
   O'er Bethlehem's midnight sky,
On man with richer promise beams,
   And lovelier scenes draw nigh.

Glad tidings of Immanuel's birth
   The angelic heralds bring;
"Glory to God, and peace on earth
   "Good will towards men," they sing.

Rise, then, my soul, and greet the morn,
   Thus sung by hosts of heaven:
For unto us a Child is born,
   To us a Son is given.

C. E.

An Advent Hymn.

"Blessed is He that cometh in the name of the Lord."—Matt. xxi, 9.

WHEN first our Lord came down on earth,
    He did not scorn like us to be,
For He was born of mortal birth,
    A simple child of low degree.

Where Syrian waves are bright and clear,
    Where Judah's grapes grow large and red,
He walked below, and men drew near
    And heard the holy words He said.

But when the Lord shall come again,
    With angel-hosts encircled round,
All earth and heaven shall hail Him then,
    With thunder peal and trumpet sound.

And some in joy and some in dread,
    The sons of men His eye shall meet;
For all the living and the dead
    Must stand before His judgment-seat.

His voice on earth we did not hear,
    His steps below we could not trace,
t when His glory shall appear,
    We too shall meet Him face to face.

For surely as the leaves and flowers
   In summer time come back again,
So surely as in sultry hours
   The dark clouds bring the pleasant rain,

Shall He who in His lowly love
   Came down that we might be forgiven,
Break, glorious, through the clouds above,
   And take His children home to heaven.
C. F. H.

When heart and flesh fail.

LOWLY and solemn be
   Thy children's cry to Thee
     Father divine!
A hymn of suppliant breath,
Owning that life and death
     Alike are Thine.

O Father, in that hour,
When earth all succouring power
   Shall disavow;
When spear, and shield, and crown,
In faintness are cast down;
   Sustain us, Thou.

By Him who bowed to take
The death-cup for our sake,

> The thorn, the rod;
> From whom the last dismay
> Was not to pass away;
> > Aid us, O God.
>
> Tremblers beside the grave,
> We call on Thee to save,
> > Father divine;
> Hear, hear our supplicant breath,
> Keep us in life and death,
> > Thine, only Thine.

Hemans.

For Christ's Sake.

"I bow my knees unto the Father of our Lord Jesus Christ, of whom the whole family in heaven and earth is named."—Eph. iii. 15.

THE quiet Sabbath sunshine played,
    With soft and loving smile,
On those in lowly church who prayed,
    And dim cathedral aisle.

There some in joy, in sorrow some,
    Beneath that sunshine knelt;
Each with his own request had come,
    Each heart its burden felt.

Yet named they all one sacred name,
    And saw one presence fair;
"For Christ our Saviour's sake,"—the same
    To each far different prayer.

While every joy, and grief, and need,
    Swelled one united cry,
Blending in Him whose name we plead,
    Our Advocate on high.

Until the soft "My God," which came
    From every praying heart,
Rose but as one "Our Father,"—name
    Which joins those far apart.

So ever, as we nearer rise
    Towards Him we all would find,
We draw more closely still the ties
    Which heart to heart can bind.

That like the union none may know,
    Of Father and of Son,
We all, who trust in Him below,
    In Him may all be one.

L. R.

Light shining out of darkness.

"Clouds and darkness are round about Him, righteousness and judgment are the habitation of His throne."—Psa. xcvii, 2.

GOD moves in a mysterious way,
   His wonders to perform;
He plants His footsteps in the sea,
   And rides upon the storm.

Deep in unfathomable mines
   Of never failing skill,
He treasures up His bright designs,
   And works His sovereign will.

Ye fearful saints, fresh courage take,
   The clouds ye so much dread
Are big with mercy, and shall break
   In blessings on your head.

Judge not the Lord by feeble sense,
   But trust Him for His grace;
Behind a frowning Providence
   He hides a smiling face.

His purposes will ripen fast,
   Unfolding every hour;
The bud may have a bitter taste,
   But sweet will be the flower.

Blind unbelief is sure to err,
    And scan His work in vain;
God is His own interpreter,
    And He will make it plain.

Cowper.

Cowper's Grave.

IT is a place where poets crowned may feel the heart's decaying;
It is a place where happy saints may weep amid their praying;
Yet let the grief and humbleness, as low as silence languish!
Earth surely now may give her calm to whom she gave her anguish.

O poets! from a maniac's tongue was poured the deathless singing;
O Christians! at your cross of hope, a hopeless hand was clinging!
O men! this man in brotherhood, your weary paths beguiling,
Groaned inly while he taught you peace, and died while you were smiling!

And now, what time ye all may read through
    dimming tears his story,
How discord on the music fell, and darkness on
    the glory,
And how, when one by one sweet sounds and
    wandering lights departed,
He wore no less a loving face because so
    broken-hearted;

He shall be strong to sanctify the poet's high
    vocation,
And bow the meekest Christian down in meeker
    adoration;
Nor ever shall he be, in praise, of wise or good
    forsaken;
Named softly as the household name of one
    whom God hath taken.

   *   *   *   *   *   *

Like a sick child that knoweth not his mother
    while she blesses,
And drops upon his burning brow the coolness
    of her kisses;
That turns his fevered eyes around—" My
    mother! where's my mother?"
As if such tender words and looks could come
    from any other!—

The fever gone, with leaps of heart, he sees
    her bending o'er him ;
Her face all pale from watchful love, the
    unweary love she bore him !—
Thus woke the poet from the dream the life-
    long fever gave him,
Beneath those deep pathetic eyes, which closed
    in death to save him !

Thus! oh not thus! no type of earth could
    image that awaking,
Wherein he scarcely heard the chant of seraphs
    round him breaking,
Or felt the new immortal throb of soul from
    body parted,
But felt *those eyes* alone, and knew "my
    Saviour, not deserted !"

Deserted? who hath dreamt that when the
    cross in darkness rested
Upon the victim's hidden face, no love was
    manifested?
What frantic hands outstretched have e'er the
    atoning drops averted?
What tears have washed them from the soul,
    that one should be deserted?

Deserted! God could separate from His own
    essence rather;
And Adam's sins *have* swept between the
    righteous Son and Father;
Yea, once Immanuel's orphaned cry His
    universe hath shaken;
It went up single, echoless, "My God, I am
    forsaken."

It went up from the Holy's lips amid His lost
    creation,
That, of the lost, no son should use those
    words of desolation;
That earth's worst phrenzies, marring hope,
    should mar not hope's fruition,
And I on Cowper's grave might see his
    rapture in a vision.
                                    E. B. Browning.

Love.

FOR the love of the true-hearted,
  Thanks we give Thee, Lord of love;
Truest treasure Thou hast given,
Fairest link 'twixt earth and heaven,
  Sunshine from above.

May this love that Thou hast given,
    Light, and hope, and joy to be ;
Filling all our lives with meaning,
Teaching truest strength in leaning,
    Draw us nearer Thee.

For the love Thou sendest shows us
    How that stronger love must glow,
By its very depth revealing
Other depths of deeper feeling
    God alone can know.

Teaching us of love unuttered,
    Ever springing, ever new,
Whose unfathomed depth and beauty
Cheer our sorrows, gild our duty,
    Perfect, constant, true.

L. R.

The Death of the Sagamore.

THE servant of God is on his way
    From Boston's beautiful shore;
The boat skims light o'er the silvery bay,
The sleeping waters awake and play
    At the touch of the splashing oar.

The boat is fast, and over the sod
    Of the neighbouring wood he hies,
Through moor and thicket his path is trod,
For he hastens to speak of the living God
    In the car of the man who dies.

The purpose that fills his soul is great
    As the heart of man may know;
Vast as eternity, strong as the gate
Which the spirit must pass to a changeless state,
    To enter on bliss or woe.

Where Romney's forest is high and dark
    The eagle lowers her wing
O'er him who once had made her his mark,
For the Sagamore, on his bed of bark,
    Is a perishing, powerless thing.

On the door of the wigwam hang the bow,
    The antlers and beavers' skin,
But he who bore them is faint and low,
For death has given the fatal blow,
    And a monarch expires within.

The eye that glanced, and the eagle fled
    Away to the fields of air;
The hand that drew, and the deer was dead;
The hunter's foot, and the chieftain's tread,
    And the conqueror's arm are there.

But each his powerful work has done,
   His triumph at length is past;
The final conflict is now begun,
And weeping the mother hangs over her son,
   As the Sagamore breathes his last.

The queen of Massachusetts grieves
   That the life of her child must end;
And that is a noble heart which heaves,
With a mortal pang, on the bed of leaves
   Of the white man's Indian friend.

That stately form that lies prostrate there,
   On those feet that are cold as snow,
Hath often sped through the midnight air,
A word to the Christian's ear to bear,
   Of the plot of his heathen foe.

And often, while roaming those wilds alone,
   His generous heart would melt,
At the touch of a ray of light which shone
From the white man's God, till before His throne
   Almost has the Indian knelt.

But the fatal fear, the fear of man,
   That brings to man a snare,
Has braced his knee, as it just began
To bend; and the fear of a heathen clan
   Has stifled the Christian's prayer.

But now like a flood to his trembling heart,
    Has the fear of a God rushed in;
And keener far than the icy dart,
That rends the flesh and spirit apart,
    Is the thought of his heathen sin.

To the lonely tent where the chief reclines,
    As the herald of love draws nigh,
The Indian shrinks, as he marks the signs
Of a soul at peace, and the light which shines
    Alone from the Christian's eye.

"Alas!" he cries, in the strange deep tone,
    Of one in the grasp of death,
"No God have I, I have lost my own,
" And I go to the presence of thine alone,
    " To scorch in His fiery breath.

" That spirit who made the sky so bright,
    " With the touch of His shining feet,
" Who rules the waters, enkindles the light,
" Imprisons the winds and gives them their
        flight,
    " I tremble His eye to meet.

" When oh, if I openly had confessed,
    " And followed and loved Him here,
" I now might fly to His arms for rest,
" Like a weary bird to her downy nest,
    " When the evening shades draw near.

" But grant me this one great boon I crave
　" In a dread and an awful hour—
" When I am gone to my lonely grave,
" Oh take my son to thy home, and save
　" This beautiful forest flower.

" To the God of thy people, the Holy One,
　" To the path that shall reach the skies;
" Say, say, that to these thou wilt lead my son,
" That he may not second the race I have run
　" Nor die as his father dies."

"As his father dies."——With the breath
　　that bore
　That sorrowful sound, hath fled
The soul of a king, for the strife is o'er
Of the spirit and flesh, and the Sagamore
　Is numbered with the dead.

But hath he not, by his high bequest,
　Like the penitent on the tree,
The Saviour of dying man confessed,
And found the promise to him addrest,
　"To-day thou shalt be with Me?"

The Lord is mindful of His own.

GOD doth not leave His own:
The night of weeping for a time may last,
   Then, tears all past,
His going forth shall as the morning shine,
The sunrise of His favour shall be thine:
   God doth not leave His own.

   God doth not leave His own;
Though few and evil all their days appear,
   Though grief and fear
Come in the train of earth and hell's dark crowd,
The trusting heart says, even in the cloud,
   God doth not leave His own.

   God doth not leave His own;
This sorrow in their life He doth permit,
   Yea, chooseth it,
To speed His children on their heavenward
     way,
He guides the winds.—Faith, hope, and
    love all say
   God doth not leave His own.

Unto us a Son is born.

HAIL to the Lord's anointed!
  Great David's greater Son!
Hail, in the time appointed,
  His reign on earth begun!
He comes to break oppression,
  To set the captive free;
To take away transgression,
  And rule in equity.

He comes with succour speedy
  For those who suffer wrong;
To help the poor and needy,
  And bid the weak be strong;
To give them songs for sighing,
  Their darkness turn to light,
Whose souls, condemned and dying,
  Were precious in His sight.

By such shall He be feared
  While sun and moon endure,
Beloved, obey'd, rever'd,
  For He shall judge the poor,
Through changing generations,
  With justice, mercy, truth,
While stars maintain their stations
  Or moons renew their youth.

He shall come down like showers
　　Upon the fruitful earth;
And love, joy, hope, like flowers,
　　Spring in His path to birth.
Before Him, on the mountains,
　　Shall Peace, the herald go;
And righteousness, in fountains,
　　From hill to valley flow.

Arabia's desert ranger
　　To Him shall bow the knee;
The Ethiopian stranger
　　His glory come to see:
With offerings of devotion,
　　Ships from the isles shall meet,
To pour the wealth of ocean
　　In tribute at His feet.

Kings shall fall down before Him,
　　And gold and incense bring;
All nations shall adore Him,
　　His praise all people sing:
For He shall have dominion
　　O'er river, sea, and shore,
Far as the eagle's pinion
　　Or dove's light wing can soar.

To Him shall prayer unceasing
　　And daily vows ascend;

His kingdom still increasing,—
  A kingdom without end.
The mountain-dew shall nourish
  A seed in weakness sown,
Whose fruit shall spread and flourish,
  And shake like Lebanon.

O'er every foe victorious,
  He on His throne shall rest;
From age to age more glorious,
  All blessing and all blest.
The tide of time shall never
  His covenant remove:
His name shall stand for ever;
  That name to us is—Love.

Montgomery.

Walk in the Light.

WALK in the light—and thou shalt own
  Thy darkness past away,
Because on thee the light hath shone
  In which is perfect day.

Walk in the light—and sin abhorred
  Shall not defile again;
The blood of Jesus Christ the Lord
  Shall cleanse from every stain.

Walk in the light—and thou shalt find
　　Thy heart made truly His,
Who dwells in cloudless light enshrined;
　　In whom no darkness is.

Walk in the light—so shalt thou know
　　That fellowship of love
His Spirit only can bestow
　　Who reigns in light above.

Walk in the light—and follow on
　　Till faith be turned to sight,
Where, in divine communion,
　　God is Himself the light.

Adoration.

ALWAY imploring palms we raise towards heaven,
　　As though we drew the consecration down:
　　And miss the holy wells that gush hard by.
　　So men mistakenly look up for dew,
　　The while its blessed mist imbathes their feet.
　　Therefore if any flower shall breathe for thee
　　A fragrant message from its pencilled urn;
　　If spring airs glad thee; if the sunset bring
　　Into thine eyes the tears of solemn joy:
　　If any radiant passion come to make
　　Existence beautiful and pure to thee;

If noblest music sway thee, like a dream;
If sorrow to a mournful midnight turn
Thy noon; if something deepest in thee wake
To a dim sentiment of mystery;
If musing warm to worship; if the stars
Earnestly beckon to immortal life;
Ponder such ministrations, and be sure
Thou hast been touched by God, O human heart.
Truman.

God in everything.

"The day is Thine, the night also is Thine, Thou hast prepared the light and the sun."—Ps. lxxv, 16.

THOU art, O God, the life and light
Of all this wondrous world we see:
Its glow by day, its smile by night,
Are but reflections caught from Thee;
Where'er we turn, Thy glories shine,
And all things fair and bright are Thine.

When day, with farewell beam, delays
Among the opening clouds of even,
And we can almost think we gaze
Through golden vistas into heaven,
Those hues, that mark the sun's decline,
So soft, so radiant, Lord, are Thine.

When youthful spring around us breathes,
Thy spirit warms her fragrant sigh,
And every flower the summer wreathes
Is born beneath that kindling eye,—
Where'er we turn, Thy glories shine,
And all things fair and bright are Thine.

Moore.

Freely ye have received, freely give.

GIVE! as the morning that flows out of heaven,
Give! as the waves when their channel is riven,
Give! as the free air and sunshine is given,
    Lavishly, utterly, carelessly give:
Not the waste drops of thy cup overflowing,
Not the faint sparks of thy hearth ever glowing,
Not a pale bud from thy June roses blowing,
    Give as He gave thee who gave thee to live.

Pour out thy love like the rush of a river
Wasting its waters for ever and ever,
Through the burnt sands that reward not the giver,
    Silent or songful thou nearest the sea.
Scatter thy life as the summer showers pouring;
What if no bird through the pearl-rain is soaring!
What if no blossom look upward adoring!
    Look to the life that was lavished for thee.

Give! though thy heart be all wasted and weary,
Laid on an altar all ashy and dreary;
Though from its pulses a faint *miserere*
    Beats to thy soul the sad presage of fate;
Bind it with cords of unshrinking devotion;
Smile at the song of its trembling emotion;
'Tis the stern hymn of eternity's ocean;
    Hear! and thy future in silence await.

So the wild wind spreads its perfumed caresses,
Evil and thankless the desert it blesses;
Bitter the wave that its soft pinion presses,
    Never it ceaseth to whisper and sing,
What if the hard heart give thorns for thy roses!
What if on rocks thy tired bosom reposes!
Sweetest is music with minor key'd closes,
    Fairest the vine that on ruins will cling.

Almost the day of thy giving is over;
Ere from the grass dies the bee-haunted clover
Thou wilt have vanished from friend and from lover:
    What shall thy longing avail in the grave?
Give, as the heart gives whose fetters are breaking,
Life, love, and hope, all thy dreams and thy waking,
Soon heaven's river thy soul-fever slaking,
    Thou shalt know God and the gift that He gave.

Forgiven.

KIND hearts are here, yet would the tenderest one
Have limits to its mercy, God has none;
And man's forgiveness may be true and sweet,
And yet he stoops to give it; more complete
Is love that lays forgiveness at thy feet
And pleads with thee to raise it: only heaven
Means crowned, not vanquished, when it says
    "Forgiven."

A. A. Procter.

Redeemed.

"There is joy in the presence of the angels of God over one sinner that repenteth."—Luke xv, 10.

    Redeemed, redeemed,
The word went forth from the Father's throne
And a flood of light from His blessed Son
    Upon the suppliant streamed;
And the angel-host, with one accord,
    Sent forth a shout and song,
For another soul by their blessed Lord
    Was promised to their throng.

    Forgiven, forgiven,
The words went up as the thunder's roll,
And on the humble trembling soul
    The echoes fell from heaven;

And the angels touched the silver strings
    Of their harps, and caught the word,
Veiled their glad faces with their wings,
    And bowed before the Lord.

    Rejoice, rejoice,
Great was the sound of joy above,
And brighter seemed the realms of love,
    Sweeter the angels' voice,
And all because one weary heart
    Had courage to be blest,
Had taken up the better part,
    And bathed its wings in rest.

Here and There.

WHAT no human eye hath seen,
    What no mortal ear hath heard,
What on thought hath never been
    In its noblest flights conferred—
This hath God prepared in store
    For His people evermore.

When the shaded pilgrim land
    Fades before my closing eye,
Then revealed on either hand
    Heaven's own scenery shall lie:

Then the veil of flesh shall fall,
    Now concealing, darkening all.

Heavenly landscapes, calmly bright,
    Life's pure river murmuring low,
Forms of loveliness and light,
    Lost to earth long time ago,—
Yes, mine own, lamented long,
    Shine amid the angel throng!

Many a joyful sight was given,
    Many a lovely vision here,
Hill, and vale, and starry even,
    Friendship's smile, affection's tear,
These were shadows sent in love,
    Of realities above!

When upon my wearied ear
    Earth's last echoes faintly die;
Then shall angel-harps draw near,
    All the chorus of the sky;
Long-hushed voices blend again,
    Sweetly in that welcome strain.

Here were sweet and varied tones,
    Bird, and breeze, and fountain's fall,
Yet creation's travail-groans
    Ever sadly sighed through all;
There no discord jars the air,
    Harmony is perfect there.

When this aching heart shall rest,
    All its busy pulses o'er,
From its mortal robes undrest
    Shall my spirit upward soar.
Then shall unimagined joy,
    All my thoughts and powers employ.

Here devotion's healing balm
    Often came to soothe my breast,
Hours of deep and holy calm,
    Earnests of eternal rest.
But the bliss was here unknown,
    Which shall there be all my own!

Jesus reigns, the Life, the Sun,
    Of that wondrous world above;
All the clouds and storms are gone,
    All is light and all is love.
All the shadows melt away
    In the blaze of perfect day!
        Hymns from the Land of Luther.

A Voice from Heaven.

I SHINE in the light of God,
    His likeness stamps my brow,
Through the shadows of death my feet have trod
    And I reign in glory now!

No breaking heart is here,
   No keen and thrilling pain,
No wasted cheek, where the frequent tear
   Hath rolled and left its stain.

I have found the joys of heaven,
   I am one of the angel band;
To my head a crown of gold is given,
   And a harp is in my hand!

I have learnt the song they sing
   Whom Jesus hath set free;
And the glorious walls of heaven still ring
   With my new-born melody.

No sin, no grief, no pain,
   Safe in my happy home!
My fears all fled, my doubts all slain,
   My hour of triumph come!

O friends of mortal years,
   The trusted and the true!
Ye are walking still in the vale of tears,
   But I wait to welcome you.

Do I forget?—Oh no!
   For memory's golden chain
Shall bind my heart to the hearts below,
   Till they meet to touch again.

Each link is strong and bright,
   And love's electric flame
Flows freely down, like a river of light,
   To the world from which I came.

Do you mourn when another star
   Shines out from the glittering sky?
Do you weep when the raging voice of war
   And the storms of conflict die?

Then, why should your tears run down,
   And your hearts be sorely riven,
For another gem in the Saviour's crown,
   And another soul in heaven?

God's-Acre.

I LIKE that ancient Saxon phrase, which calls
   The burial ground God's-Acre! It is just;
It consecrates each grave within its walls,
   And breathes a benison o'er the sleeping dust.

God's-Acre! Yes, that blessed name imparts
   Comfort to those who in the grave have sown
The seed that they have garnered in their hearts,
   Their bread of life; alas! no more their own.

Into its furrows shall we all be cast,
  In the sure faith that we shall rise again
At the great harvest, when the archangel's blast
  Shall winnow, like a fan, the chaff and grain.

Then shall the good stand in immortal bloom,
  In the fair gardens of that second birth;
And each bright blossom mingle its perfume
  With that of flowers which never bloomed on earth.

With thy rude ploughshare, Death, turn up the sod,
  And spread the furrow for the seed we sow;
This is the field and acre of our God,
  This is the place where human harvests grow!
Longfellow.

The Dream.

WEARIED and worn with earthly cares, I
    yielded to repose,
And soon before my raptured sight, a glorious
    vision rose:
  I thought, whilst slumbering on my couch in
    midnight's silent gloom,
  I heard an angel's silvery voice, and radiance
    filled my room.

A gentle touch awakened me,—a gentle whisper said,
"Arise, O sleeper, follow me;" and thro' the air we fled.
We left the earth so far away that like a speck it seemed,
And heavenly glory, calm and pure, across our pathway streamed.

Still on we went,—my soul was wrapt in silent ecstacy;
I wondered what the end would be, what next should meet mine eye.
I knew not how we journeyed thro' the pathless fields of light,
When suddenly a change was wrought, and I was clothed in white.

We stood before a city's walls, most glorious to behold;
We passed thro' gates of glistening pearl, o'er streets of purest gold;
It needed not the sun by day, the silver moon by night;
The glory of the Lord was there, the Lamb Himself its light.

Bright angels paced the shining streets, sweet music filled the air,
And white-robed saints, with glittering crowns, from every clime were there!

And some that I had loved on earth stood
    with them round the throne,
"All worthy is the Lamb," they sang, "the
    glory His alone."

But fairer far than all beside, I saw my
    Saviour's face;
And as I gazed, He smiled on me with
    wondrous love and grace.
Lowly I bowed before His throne, o'erjoyed
    that I at last
Had gained the object of my hopes, that
    earth at length was past.

And then in solemn tones He said, "Where
    is the diadem
"That should be sparkling on thy brow
    adorned with many a gem?
"I know thou hast believed on Me, and life
    through Me is thine;
"But where are all those radiant stars that
    in thy crown should shine?

"Thou seest now yonder glorious throng,
    the stars on every brow!
"For every soul they led to Me, they wear a
    jewel now!
"And such thy bright reward had been, if
    such had been thy deed,
"If thou hadst sought some wand'ring feet
    in path of peace to lead.

"I did not mean that thou should'st tread
    the way of life alone,
"But that the clear and shining light, which
    round thy footsteps shone,
"Should guide some other weary feet to my
    bright home of rest,
"And thus in blessing those around, thou
    hadst thyself been blest."

* * * * * *

The vision faded from my sight, the voice
    no longer spake,
A spell seemed brooding o'er my soul which
    long I feared to break;
And when at last I gazed around in
    morning's glimmering light,
My spirit fell o'erwhelmed beneath that
    vision's awful might.

I rose and wept with chastened joy, that
    yet I dwelt below;
That yet another hour was mine, my faith
    by works to shew;
That yet some sinner I might tell of Jesus'
    dying love,
And help to lead some weary soul to seek a
    home above.

And now while on the earth I stay, my
    motto this shall be,
"To live no longer to myself, but Him who
    died for me;"
And graven on my inmost soul this word of
    truth divine,
"They that turn many to the Lord bright
    as the stars shall shine."
S. S. Treasury.

Sleep.

WHEN in the silvery moonlight
    The lengthen'd shadows fall,
And the silence of night is dropping
    Like the gentle dew on all;

When the river's tranquil murmur
    Doth lulling cadence keep,
And blossoms close their weary eyes,
    He giveth all things sleep.

From the little bud of the daisy,
    And the young bird in the nest,
To the humble bed of the peasant child,
    All share that quiet rest.

It comes to the poor man's garret,
    And the captive's lonely cell:
On the sick man's tossing, feverish couch,
    It lays a blessed spell.

And the Holy One who sends it down,
    For a healing and a balm,
Doth bless it with a mighty power
    Of peacefulness and calm.

He counts the buds that fade and droop,
    And marks all those who weep;
And closes weary, aching eyes,
    With the holy kiss of sleep:

The truest comfort He has given
    For all earth's pain and woe,
Until that glorious life beyond
    Nor tears nor sleep shall know.

Mrs. Broderip.

Bless us to-night.

FATHER of love and power,
Guard Thou our evening hour,
    Shield with Thy might.
For all Thy care this day
Our grateful thanks we pay,
And to our Father pray,
    Bless us to-night.

Jesus Emmanuel,
Come in Thy love to dwell
    In hearts contrite;

For many sins we grieve,
But we Thy grace receive,
And in Thy word believe,
　　Bless us to-night.

Spirit of truth and love,
Life-giving holy Dove,
　　Shed forth Thy light;
Heal every sinner's smart,
Still every throbbing heart,
And Thine own peace impart.
　　Bless us to-night.

A Psalm of Life.

TELL me not, in mournful numbers,
　　Life is but an empty dream;
For the soul is dead that slumbers,
　　And things are not what they seem.

Life is real! life is earnest!
　　And the grave is not its goal;
"Dust thou art, to dust returnest,"
　　Was not spoken of the soul.

Not enjoyment, and not sorrow,
　　Is our destined end or way;
But to act, that each to-morrow
　　Find us farther than to-day.

Art is long, and time is fleeting,
    And our hearts, though stout and brave,
Still, like muffled drums, are beating
    Funeral marches to the grave.

In the world's broad field of battle,
    In the bivouac of life,
Be not like dumb, driven cattle!
    Be a hero in the strife!

Trust no future, howe'er pleasant!
    Let the dead past bury its dead!
Act,—act in the living present!
    Heart within, and God o'erhead!

Lives of great men all remind us
    We can make our lives sublime,
And departing leave behind us
    Footprints on the sands of time:

Footprints, that perhaps another,
    Sailing o'er life's solemn main,
A forlorn and shipwrecked brother,
    Seeing, shall take heart again.

Let us, then, be up and doing,
    With a heart for any fate;
Still achieving, still pursuing,
    Learn to labour and to wait.

Longfellow.

The Hours.

THE hours are viewless angels,
    That still go gliding by,
And bear each minute's record up
    To Him who sits on high;
And we, who walk among them,
    As one by one departs,
See not that they are hovering
    For ever round our hearts.

Like summer-bees, that hover
    Around the idle flowers,
They gather every act and thought,
    Those viewless angel-hours;
The poison or the nectar
    The heart's deep flower-cups yield,
A sample still they gather swift
    And leave us in the field.

And some flit by on pinions
    Of joyous gold and blue,
And some flag on with drooping wings
    Of sorrow's darker hue;
But still they steal the record,
    And bear it far away:
Their mission-flight, by day or night
    No magic power can stay.

And as we spend each minute
  That God to us hath given,
The deeds are known before His throne,
  The tale is told in heaven.
Those bee-like hours we see not,
  Nor hear their noiseless wings;
We often feel, too oft, when flown,
  That they have left their stings.

So teach me, heavenly Father,
  To meet each flying hour,
That as they go they may not show
  My heart a poison flower!
So! when death brings its shadows
  The hours that linger last
Shall bear my hopes on angel wings,
  Unfetter'd by the past.

C. P. *Cranch.*

Silence.

IN silence mighty things are wrought—
Silently builded, thought on thought,
  Truth's temple greets the sky;
And like a citadel with towers,
The soul with her subservient powers
  Is strengthened silently.

Soundless as chariots on the snow
The saplings of the forest grow
  To trees of mighty girth;
Each nightly star in silence burns,
And every day in silence turns
  The axle of the earth.

The silent frost with mighty hand
Fetters the rivers and the land
  With universal chain;
And, smitten by the silent sun,
The chain is loosed, the rivers run,
  The lands are free again.

O Source unseen of life and light,
Thy secrecy of silent might
  If we in bondage know,
Our hearts, like seeds beneath the ground,
By silent force of life unbound,
  Move upward from below.

T. T. Lynch.

Open Thou our eyes.

"Jesus Himself drew near and went with them"—Luke xxiv.

AND He drew near and talked with them,
  But they perceived Him not,
And mourned, unconscious of that light—
  The gloom, the darkness, and the night
    That wrapt His burial spot.

Wearied with doubt, perplexed, and sad,
   They knew nor help, nor guide,
While He who bore the secret key
To open every mystery,
   Unknown was by their side.

Thus often when we feel alone,
   No help nor comfort near,
'Tis only that our eyes are dim,
Doubting and sad we see not Him
   Who waiteth still to hear.

"The darkness gathers overhead,
   "The morn will never come,"
Did we but raise our down-cast eyes,
In the wide-flushing eastern skies
   Appears the glowing sun.

In all our daily joys and griefs,
   In daily work and rest,
To those who seek Him, Christ is near,
Our bliss to calm, to soothe our care,
   In leaning on His breast.

Open our eyes, O Lord, we pray,
   To see our way—our Guide,
That by the path that here we tread,
We following on may still be led
   In Thy light to abide.

L. R.

Discouraged because of the way.

THE way seems dark about me—overhead
The clouds have long since met in gloomy spread,
And when I looked to see the day break through,
Cloud after cloud came up with volume new.

And in that shadow I have passed along
Feeling myself grow weak as it grew strong,
Walking in doubt, and searching for the way,
And often at a stand—as now to-day.

And if before me on the path there lies
A spot of brightness from imagined skies,
Imagined shadows fall across it too,
And the far future takes the present's hue.

Perplexities do throng upon my sight,
Like scudding fog-banks, to obscure the light;
Some new dilemma rises every day,
And I can only shut my eyes and pray.

Lord, I am not sufficient for these things,
Give me the light that Thy sweet presence brings;
Give me Thy grace, give me Thy constant strength:
Lord, for my comfort now appear at length.

It may be that my way doth seem confused,
Because my heart of Thy way is afraid;
Because my eyes have constantly refused
To see the only opening Thou hast made.

Because my will would cross some flowery plain
Where Thou hast thrown a hedge from side to side;
And turneth from the stony walk of pain,
Its trouble or its ease not even tried.

If thus I try to force my way along—
The smoothest road encumbered is for me;
For were I as an angel swift and strong,
I could not go unless allowed by Thee.

And now I pray Thee, Lord, to lead Thy child—
Poor wretched wanderer from Thy grace and love;
Whatever way Thou pleasest through the wild,
So it but take her to Thy home above.

When I am weak, then am I strong.

HALF feeling our own weakness
    We place our hands in Thine,—
Knowing but half our darkness
    We ask for light divine.

Then, when Thy strong arm holds us,
    Our weakness most we feel,
And Thy love-light around us
    Our darkness doth reveal.

Too oft, when faithless doubtings
    Around our spirits press,
We cry, "Can hands so feeble
    "Grasp such almightiness?"

While thus we doubt and tremble,
  Our hold still looser grows;
While on our darkness gazing
  Vainly Thy radiance glows.

Oh! cheer us with Thy brightness,
  And guide us by Thy hand,
In Thy light teach us light to see,
  In Thy strength strong to stand.

Then though our hands be feeble,
  If they but touch Thine arm,
Thy light and power shall lead us
  And keep us strong and calm.

Rock of Ages.

ROCK of ages, cleft for me,
  Let me hide myself in Thee.
  Let the water and the blood,
From Thy wounded side which flowed,
  Be of sin the double cure,
  Cleanse me from its guilt and power.

Not the labour of my hands
Can fulfil Thy law's demands.
Could my zeal no respite know,
Could my tears for ever flow,
  All for sin could not atone;
  Thou must save, and Thou alone.

Nothing in my hand I bring,
Simply to Thy cross I cling;
Naked, come to Thee for dress;
Helpless, look to Thee for grace;
Black, I to the fountain fly;
Wash me, Saviour, or I die.

While I draw this fleeting breath,
When my eyelids close in death,
When I soar to worlds unknown,
See Thee on Thy judgment throne,
Rock of ages, shelter me,
Let me hide myself in Thee.

Toplady.

Faith in Christ.

MY faith looks up to Thee,
Thou Lamb of Calvary,
    Saviour Divine.
Now hear me while I pray,
Take all my guilt away,
Oh let me from this day
    Be wholly Thine.

May Thy rich grace impart
Strength to my fainting heart,
    My zeal inspire,
As Thou hast died for me,
Oh may my love to Thee
Pure, warm, and changeless be,
    A living fire.

While life's dark maze I tread,
And griefs around me spread,
   Be Thou my guide,
Bid darkness turn to day,
Wipe sorrow's tears away,
Nor let me ever stray
   From Thee aside.

When ends life's transient dream,
When death's cold sullen stream
   Shall o'er me roll;
Dear Saviour, then in love
Fear and distrust remove,
And bear me safe above,
   A ransomed soul.

Look to Jesus.

JESUS in Thy memory keep,
 Wouldst thou be God's child and friend;
Jesus in thy heart shrined deep,
 Still thy gaze on Jesus bend,
In thy toiling, in thy resting,
Look to Him with every breath,
Look to Jesus' life and death.

Look to Jesus, till, reviving,
 Faith and love thy life-springs swell,
Strength for all things good deriving
 From Him who did all things well;

Work, as He did, in thy season,
Works which shall not fade away,
Work while it is called to-day.

Look to Jesus, prayerful, waking,
    When thy feet on roses tread;
Follow, worldly pomp forsaking,
    With thy cross, where He hath led.
Look to Jesus in temptation;
Baffled shall the tempter flee,
And God's angels come to thee.

Look to Jesus when dark lowering
    Perils thy horizon dim,
By that band in terror cowering,
    Calm midst tempests, look to Him.
Trust in Him who still rebuketh
Wind and billow, fire and flood;
Forward! brave by trusting God.

Look to Jesus, when distressèd
    See what He, the Holy, bore;
Is thy heart with conflict pressèd?
    Is thy soul still harass'd sore?
See His sweat of blood, His conflict,
Watch His agony increase,
Hear His prayer, and feel His peace!

Franzén.

Jesus.

THERE is a name I love to hear,
    I love to speak its worth;
It sounds like music in mine ear,
    The sweetest name on earth.

It tells me of a Saviour's love,
    Who died to set me free;
It tells me of His precious blood,
    The sinner's perfect plea.

It tells me of a Father's smile
    Beaming upon His child,
It cheers me through this "little while,"
    Through desert, waste, and wild.

It tells me what my Father hath
    In store for every day,
And though I tread a darksome path,
    Yields sunshine all the way.

It tells of One whose loving heart
    Can feel my deepest woe,
Who in my sorrow bears a part,
    That none can bear below.

It bids my trembling soul rejoice,
    It dries each rising tear;
It tells me in a "still small voice,"
    To trust and not to fear.

Jesus! the name I love so well,
    The name I love to hear!
No saint on earth its worth can tell,
    No heart conceive how dear.

This name shall shed its fragrance still
    Along this thorny road;
Shall sweetly smooth the rugged hill
    That leads me up to God.

And there, with all the blood-bought throng,
    From sin and sorrow free,
I'll sing the new eternal song
    Of Jesus' love for me.

F. W.

A City that hath foundations.

BEYOND the dark and stormy bound
That girds our dull horizon round,
    A lovelier landscape swells;
Resplendent seat of light and peace,
In thee the sounds of conflict cease,
    And glory ever dwells.

For thee the early patriarch sighed,
Thy distant beauty faint descried,
    And hailed the blessed abode;
A stranger here, he sought a home
Fixed in a city yet to come,
    The city of his God.

Oft by Siloa's sacred stream,
In heavenly trance and raptured dream,
  To faithful Israel shewn,
Triumphant over all her foes,
The true celestial Salem rose,
  Jehovah's promised throne.

We too, O Lord, would seek that land,
Follow the tribes that crowd its strand,
  From every peril saved;
And wake as when, in elder time,
Were marshalled all Thy hosts sublime,
  And high Thy banner waved.

Sabbath.

AFTER long days of storm and showers,
    Of sighing winds and dripping bowers,
  How sweet at morn to ope our eyes
    On newly swept and garnished skies.

To miss the cloud and driving rain,
  And see that all is bright again,
So bright we cannot choose but say,
  "Is this the world of yesterday?"

E'en so methinks, the Sabbath brings
  A change o'er all familiar things;
A change we know not whence it came,
  They are, and they are not the same.

There is a spell within, around,
　　On eye and ear, on sight and sound,
And, loth or willing, they and we
　　Must own this day a mystery.

Sure all things wear a heavenly dress,
　　Which sanctifies their loveliness;
Types of that endless resting day,
　　When we shall all be changed as they.

To-day our peaceful, ordered home,
　　Foreshadoweth mansions yet to come,
We foretaste, in domestic love,
　　The faultless charities above.

And as at yester eventide
　　Our tasks and toys were laid aside,
So here, we're training for the day
　　When we shall lay them down for aye.

But not alone for musing deep,
　　Our souls this "day of days" would keep,
Yet other glorious things than these,
　　The Christian in his sabbath sees.

His eyes by faith his Lord behold,
　　How on the week's "first day" of old
From hell He rose, on earth He trod,
　　Was seen of men, and went to God.

And as we fondly pause to look,
　When in some daily-handled book,
Approval's well-known tokens stand,
　Traced by some dear and thoughtful hand;

E'en so there shines one day in seven,
　Bright with the special mark of heaven,
That we with love and praise may dwell
　On Him who loveth us so well.

Whether in meditative walk
　Alone with God and heaven we talk,
Catching the simple chime which calls
　Our feet to some old church's walls,—

Or passed within the church's door,
　Where poor are rich, and rich are poor,
We pray the prayers, and hear the word,
　Which there our fathers prayed and heard.

Or represent in solemn wise,
　Our all-prevailing Sacrifice,
Feeding in communion high
　The life of faith which cannot die.

And surely in a world like this,
　So rife with woe, so scant of bliss,
Where fondest hopes are often crossed,
　And fondest hearts are severed most,—

'Tis something that we kneel and pray,
    With loved ones near and far away,
One God, one faith, one hope, one care,
    One form of words, one hour of prayer.

'Tis past, yet pause till ear and heart,
    In one brief silence ere we part,
Something of that high strain have caught,
    The peace of God which passeth aught.

Then turn we to our earthly homes,
    Not doubting but that Jesus comes,
Breathing His peace on hall and hut,
    "At even when the doors are shut,"—

Then speeds us on our earthly way,
    And hallows every common day,
Without Him Sunday's self were dim,
    And all are bright if spent with Him.

Quiet from God.

QUIET from God, it cometh not to still
The vast and high aspirings of the soul,
The deep emotions that the spirit fill,
And speed its purpose onward to the goal.
    It dims not youth's bright eye,
    Bend not joy's lofty brow;
    No guileless ecstasy
    Need in its presence bow.

It comes not in a sullen form to place
Life's greatest good in an inglorious rest,
Through a dull beaten track its way to trace,
And to lethargic slumber lull the breast.
  Action may be its sphere,
  Mountain paths, boundless fields,
  O'er billows its career;
  This is the strength it yields.

To sojourn in the world and yet apart,
To dwell with God, and yet with man to feel,
To bear about for ever in the heart
The gladness that His spirit doth reveal.
  Not to deem evil gone
  From every earthly scene,
  To see the storm come on
  But feel His shield between.

It giveth not a power to human kind
To lay all suffering powerless at its feet,
But keeps within the temple of the mind
A golden altar and a mercy seat,
  A spiritual ark,
  Bearing the peace of God
  Above the waters dark
  And o'er the desert sod.

How beautiful within our souls to keep,
This treasure the All-merciful hath given,
To feel when we awake and when we sleep
Its incense round us like a breath from heaven,

    Quiet at heart and home,
    Where the heart's joys begin,
    Quiet where'er we roam,
    Quiet around, within.

What shall make trouble? not the adverse minds
That like a shadow o'er creation lower,
The spirit peace hath so attunèd, finds
There feelings that may own the Calmer's power.
    What may she not confer,
    E'en whilst she must condemn?
    They take not peace from her,
    She may speak peace to them.

What shall make trouble? not an adverse fate,
Not chilling poverty or worldly care,
They who are tending to a better state
Want but that peace to make them feel they are;
    Care o'er life's little day
    The tempest-clouds may roll,
    Peace o'er its eve shall play,
    The moonlight of the soul.

What shall make trouble? not the holy thought
Of the departed—that shall be a part
Of the undying things that peace hath wrought
Into a world of beauty in the heart.
    Not the forms passed away
    That life's strong current bore,
    Though the stream might not stay
    The ocean shall restore.

What shall make trouble? not slow wasting pain,
Not the impending, certain stroke of death:
These do but wear away, then snap, the chain
That binds the spirit down to things beneath,
  The quiet of the grave
  No trouble can destroy,
  He who is strong to save
  Shall break it but with joy.

"Beyond."

WE must not doubt, or fear, or dread, that
  love for life is only given,
And that the calm and sainted dead will
  meet estranged and cold in heaven:—
Oh! love were poor and vain indeed, based
  on so harsh and stern a creed.

True that this earth must pass away, with all
  the starry worlds of light,
With all the glory of the day, and calmer
  tenderness of night;
For, in that radiant home can shine alone
  the immortal and divine.

Earth's lower things—her pride, her fame, her
    science, learning, wealth, and power,
Slow growths, that through long ages came, or
    fruits of some convulsive hour,
Whose very memory must decay—heaven is too
    pure for such as they.

They are complete: their work is done. So let
    them sleep in endless rest;
Love's life is only here begun, nor is, nor can
    be, fully blest;
It has no room to spread its wings, amid this
    crowd of meaner things.

Just for the very shadow thrown upon its sweet-
    ness here below,
The cross that it must bear alone, and bloody
    baptism of woe,
Crowned and completed through its pain, we
    know that it shall rise again.

So if its flame burn pure and bright, here, where
    our air is dark and dense,
And nothing in this world of night lives with
    a living so intense;
When it shall reach its home at length—how
    bright its light! how strong its strength!

And while the vain weak loves of earth (for such
 base counterfeits abound)
Shall perish with what gave them birth, their
 graves are green and fresh around,
No funeral song shall need to rise, for the true
 love that never dies.

If in my heart I now could fear that, risen
 again, we should not know
What was our life of life when here—the hearts
 we loved so much below ;
I would arise this very day, and cast so poor a
 thing away.

But love is no such soulless clod : living,
 perfected it shall rise
Transfigured in the light of God, and giving
 glory to the skies :
And that which makes this life so sweet, shall
 render heaven's joy complete.
A. A. Procter.

Living.

AFTER A DEATH.

"That friend of mine who lives in God."

H live !
(Thus seems it we should say to our beloved,
Each held by such slight links so oft removed :)
And I can let thee go to the world's end ;
All precious names, companion, love, spouse, friend,

Seal up in an eternal silence grey,
Like a closed grave till resurrection-day:
All sweet remembrances, hopes, dreams, desires,
Heap, as one heaps up sacrificial fires;
Then turning, consecrate by loss, and proud
Of penury—go back into the loud
Tumultuous world again with never a moan,
Save that which whispers still, " My own, my own,"
Under the same broad sky whose arch immense
Enfolds us both like the arm of Providence:
And thus contented I could live or die,
With never clasp of hand or meeting eye
On this side Paradise.—While thee I see
Living to God, thou art alive to me.

O live!
And I, methinks, can let all dear rights go,
Fond duties melt away like April snow,
And sweet, sweet hopes, that took a life to weave,
Vanish like gossamers of autumn eve.
Nay, sometimes seems it I could even bear
To lay down humbly this love-crown I wear,
Steal from my palace, helpless, hopeless, poor,
And see another queen it at the door—
If only that the king had done no wrong,
If this my palace, where I dwelt so long,
Were not defiled by falsehood entering in:
There is no loss but change, no death but sin,
No parting, save the slow corrupting pain
Of murdered faith that never lives again.

Oh live!
(So endeth faint the low pathetic cry
Of love, whom death hath taught, love cannot die)
And I can stand above the daisy bed,
The only pillow for thy dearest head,
There cover up for ever from my sight
My own, my own, my all of earth-delight;
And enter the sea-cave of widowed years,
Where far, far off the trembling gleam appears
Through which thy heavenly image slipped away,
And waits to meet me at the open day.
Only to me, my love, only to me
This cavern underneath the moaning sea;
This long, long life that I alone must tread,
To whom the living seem most like the dead,
Thou wilt be safe out on the happy shore:
He who in God lives, liveth evermore.

Poems by the Author of "John Halifax."

For ever with the Lord.

SWEET home echo on the pilgrim's way,
   Thrice welcome message from a land of light,
As through a clouded sky the moonbeams stray,
   So on eternity's deep shrouded night
Streams a mild radiance, from that cheering word,
   "So shall we be for ever with the Lord."

At home with Jesus! He who went before,
　　For His own people mansions to prepare;
The soul's deep longings stilled, its conflicts o'er,
　　All rest and blessedness with Jesus there.—
What home like this can the wide earth afford?
　　"So shall we be for ever with the Lord."

With Him all gathered! to that blessed home
　　Through all its windings, still the pathway tends;
While ever and anon bright glimpses come
　　Of that fair city where the journey ends.
Where all of bliss is centred in one word,
　　"So shall we be for ever with the Lord."

Here, kindred hearts are severed far and wide,
　　By many a weary mile of land and sea,
Or life's all varied cares, and paths divide;—
　　But yet a joyful gathering shall be,
The broken links repaired, the lost restored,
　　"So shall we be for ever with the Lord."

And is there ever perfect union here?
　　Oh! daily sins lamented and confessed,
They come between us and the friends most dear,
　　They mar our blessedness and break our rest.
With life we leave the evils long deplored,
　　"So shall we be for ever with the Lord."

All prone to error—none set wholly free
  From the old serpent's soul-ensnaring chain,
The truths one child of God can clearly see,
  He seeks to make his brother feel in vain;
But all shall harmonize in heaven's full chord,
  "So shall we be for ever with the Lord."

O precious promise, mercifully given,
  Well may it hush the wail of earthly woe;
O'er the dark passage to the gates of heaven,
  The light of hope and resurrection throw.
Thanks for the blessed, life-inspiring word,
  "So shall we be for ever with the Lord."

Hymns from the Land of Luther.

Morning.

"His compassions fail not. They are new every morning."—Lam. iii. 22, 23.

CUES of the rich unfolding morn,
That, ere the glorious sun be born,
  By some soft touch invisible
  Around his path are taught to swell;—

Thou rustling breeze so fresh and gay,
That danceth forth at opening day,
  And brushing by with joyous wing,
  Wakenest each little leaf to sing;—

Ye fragrant clouds of dewy steam,
By which deep grove and tangled stream
Pay, for soft rains in season given,
Their tribute to the genial heaven;—

Why waste your treasures of delight
Upon our thankless, joyless sight;
Who day by day to sin awake,
Seldom of heaven and you partake?

Oh! timely happy, timely wise,
Hearts that with rising morn arise!
Eyes that the beam celestial view,
Which evermore makes all things new!

New every morning is the love
Our wakening and uprising prove;
Through sleep and darkness safely brought,
Restored to life, and power, and thought.

New mercies, each returning day,
Hover around us while we pray;
New perils past, new sins forgiven,
New thoughts of God, new hopes of heaven.

If in our daily course our mind
Be set to hallow all we find,
New treasures still, of countless price,
God will provide for sacrifice.

Old friends, old scenes, will lovelier be,
As more of heaven in each we see:
Some softening gleam of love and prayer
Shall dawn on every cross and care.

As for some dear familiar strain
Untir'd we ask, and ask again,
Ever, in its melodious store,
Finding a spell unheard before;

Such is the bliss of souls serene,
When they have sworn, and steadfast mean,
Counting the cost, in all to' espy
Their God, in all themselves deny.

O could we learn that sacrifice,
What lights would all around us rise!
How would our hearts with wisdom talk
Along life's dullest dreariest walk!

We need not bid, for cloister'd cell,
Our neighbour and our work farewell,
Nor strive to wind ourselves too high
For sinful man beneath the sky:

The trivial round, the common task,
Would furnish all we ought to ask;
Room to deny ourselves; a road
To bring us, daily, nearer God.

Seek we no more; content with these,
Let present rapture, comfort, ease,
As heaven shall bid them, come and go:—
The secret this of rest below.

Only, O Lord, in Thy dear love
Fit us for perfect rest above;
And help us, this and every day,
To live more nearly as we pray.
Christian Year.

Evening.

"Abide with us, for it is toward evening, and the day is far spent."—Luke xxiv, 29.

'TIS gone, that bright and orbèd blaze,
Fast fading from our wistful gaze;
Yon mantling cloud has hid from sight
The last faint pulse of quivering light.

In darkness and in weariness
The traveller on his way must press,
No gleam to watch on tree or tower,
Whiling away the lonesome hour.

Sun of my soul! Thou Saviour dear,
It is not night if Thou be near:
Oh! may no earth-born cloud arise
To hide Thee from Thy servant's eyes.

When round Thy wondrous works below
My searching rapturous glance I throw,
Tracing out wisdom, power, and love,
In earth or sky, in stream or grove;

Or by the light Thy words disclose
Watch time's full river as it flows,
Scanning Thy gracious providence,
Where not too deep for mortal sense:—

When with dear friends sweet talk I hold,
And all the flowers of life unfold;
Let not my heart within me burn,
Except in all I Thee discern.

When the soft dews of kindly sleep
My wearied eyelids gently steep,
Be my last thought, how sweet to rest
For ever on my Saviour's breast.

Abide with me from morn till eve,
For without Thee I cannot live:
Abide with me when night is nigh,
For without Thee I dare not die.

Thou framer of the light and dark,
Steer through the tempest Thine own ark:
Amid the howling wintry sea
We are in port if we have Thee.

Oh! by Thine own sad burthen, borne
So meekly up the hill of scorn,
Teach Thou Thy priests their daily cross
To bear as Thine, nor count it loss!

If some poor wandering child of Thine
Have spurn'd, to-day, the voice divine,
Now, Lord, the gracious work begin;
Let him no more lie down in sin.

Watch by the sick: enrich the poor
With blessings from Thy boundless store:
Be every mourner's sleep to-night
Like infant's slumbers, pure and light.

Come near and bless us when we wake,
Ere through the world our way we take;
Till in the ocean of Thy love
We lose ourselves in heaven above.

Christian Year.

Index.

	PAGE.
Abide with me; fast falls the eventide	31
After long days of storm and showers	195
Ah! not alone the murderous blade	36
A little brook went singing	47
A little cloud was fashioned	6
All night the lonely suppliant prayed	18
Alway imploring palms we raise toward heaven	165
And He drew near and talked with them	185
As the harp strings only render	131
As those that watch for the day	73
Beyond the dark and stormy bound	194
Birds have their quiet nest	105
Calm on the bosom of thy God	92
Christ, whose glory fills the skies	82
Come, my soul, awake, 'tis morning	138
Cometh sunshine after rain	123
Commit thou all thy griefs	29
Commit thy way to God	68
Count not the days that have idly flown	65
Faith, hope, charity—these three	45
Father and Friend! Thy light, Thy love	52
Father I bring this worthless child to Thee	106
Father, I know that all my life	25
Father of love and power	180
Father, Thy will, not mine, be done	123
Father! whate'er of earthly bliss	67

INDEX.

	PAGE.
For ever with the Lord!	94
For the love of the true-hearted	155
Forth from the dark and stormy sky	85
Give as the morning that flows out of heaven!	167
Glorious things of thee are spoken	102
Glorious was that primeval light	146
Go when the morning shineth	86
God be with thee my beloved, God be with thee!	30
God doth not leave His own	161
God moves in a mysterious way	151
Gracious spirit, dwell with me	110
Hail to the Lord's Anointed	162
Half feeling our own weakness	188
Hast thou not seen at break of day	15
Heavenward doth our journey tend	60
Holy Saviour, Friend unseen	132
Hues of the rich unfolding morn	207
I am old and blind	27
I have a wondrous house to build	62
I heard the voice of Jesus say	142
I hoped that with the brave and strong	70
I like that ancient Saxon phrase, which calls	174
In silence mighty things are wrought	184
In the mid silence of the voiceless night	136
I shine in the light of God	172
It came upon the midnight clear	78
It is a place where poets crowned may feel the heart's decaying	152
Jesus in thy memory keep	191
Judge not; the workings of his brain	44
Just as I am, without one plea	88
Kind hearts are here, yet would the tenderest one	169
Light of lights, enlighten me	119
Lord, and what shall this man do?	22
Lord I am come alone with Thee	121
Lord! we sit and cry to Thee	83
Lord, what a change within us one short hour	87
"Lovest thou me?" I hear my Saviour say	112
Lowly and solemn be	143

INDEX.

	PAGE.
Much have I borne, but not as I should bear	133
My God I thank Thee who hast made	134
My faith looks up to Thee	190
Nearer, my God, to Thee	129
Never hasting, never resting	13
Nothing resting in its own completeness	127
Not in the solitude	50
Nought see we here as yet in full perfection	17
Of all the thoughts of God that are	1
Oh for a heart to praise my God	109
Oh live! Thus seems it we should say to our beloved	203
Oh talk to me of heaven, I love	93
O sweet home echo on the pilgrim's way	205
Once slow and sad the evening fell	113
One sweetly solemn thought	89
Onward! the goal thou seekest	12
Pleasant are Thy courts above	114
Quiet from God! it cometh not to still	193
Redeemed, redeemed!	169
Robin, to the bare bough clinging	80
Rock of ages, cleft for me	189
Saviour divine, we bend before Thee lowly	108
Saviour of men, and Lord of love	104
See! the dull dense clouds are breaking	74
She, 'neath ice-mountains vast	34
Sold by them that should have loved thee	143
Some murmur when their sky is clear	136
Songs of praise the angels sang	125
Source of my life's refreshing springs	21
Speak gently! it is better far	41
Still evermore for some great strength we pray	39
Still nigh me, O my Saviour, stand	112
Strive; yet I do not promise	20
Sweet brooklet! ever gliding	52
Take them, O Death, and bear away	23
Tell me not, in mournful numbers	181
The baby wept	92
The blue Egean's countless waves in Sabbath sunlight smiled	116

INDEX.

	PAGE.
The golden morn flames up the eastern sky	54
The hours are viewless angels	183
The ivy in a dungeon grew	10
The last sand from Time's hour glass	59
The quiet Sabbath sunshine played	149
The servant of God is on his way	156
The way seems dark about me, overhead	187
There is a name I love to hear	193
They came, they went: of pleasures passed away	17
Think gently of the erring	42
This world I deem	56
Thou art, O God, the life and light	166
Thou, who didst stoop below	84
Throughout this earth in stillness	126
Thy love shall chant itself its own beatitudes	39
Thy way, not mine, O Lord	66
'Tis gone, that bright and orbèd blaze	210
'Twas long ago in olden time	140
Under the bowering honeysuckle	45
Walk in the light and thou shalt own	164
We ask for peace, O Lord!	3
We love Thee, Lord, yet not alone	71
We must not doubt, or fear, or dread, that love for life is only given	201
We seek that land whose light e'en now	98
We would see Jesus, for the shadows lengthen	90
Wearied and worn with earthly cares, I yielded to repose	175
What must it be to dwell above	100
What no human eye hath seen	170
What sudden blaze of song	76
When first our Lord came down on earth	147
When in the silvery moonlight	179
When prayer delights thee least, then learn to say	5
Whither, midst falling dew	33
Who shall ascend to the holy place?	101
Ye dainty mosses, lichens grey	24

J. FLETCHER, PRINTER, NORWICH.

www.ingramcontent.com/pod-product-compliance
Lightning Source LLC
Chambersburg PA
CBHW021841230426
43669CB00008B/1042